D1260161

SAINTS AND LEADERS

SAINTS AND LEADERS

BY THE

REV. H. F. B. MACKAY

AUTHOR OF "THE MESSAGE OF FRANCIS OF ASSISI"
"ASSISTANTS AT THE PASSION"

LONDON

PHILIP ALLAN & CO., LTD.

QUALITY HOUSE, GREAT RUSSELL STREET, W.C.1

First Published - - - *June,* 1928
Second Impression - *December,* 1928
Third Impression- - *December,* 1929

Printed in Great Britain
at the BURLEIGH PRESS, *Lewin's Mead,* BRISTOL.

PREFATORY NOTE

THIS collection of addresses merely represents the attempt of a very busy London incumbent to bring his congregation to look with him at some of the great figures of the past.

The addresses were all given in All Saints' Church, Margaret Street, with the exception of the paper on Dr. Johnson's Religion, which was read to an Oxford Essay Society. Here are two addresses on St. Cyprian, one on St. Athanasius, a series on St. Jerome, another on St. Ambrose, and yet another on some worthies of our later English Church.

I have ventured to collect them because I have been told that they may be useful for reading at retreat meals. The choice of a book for the refectory is not always easy and has been sometimes unfortunate. I have revengeful memories of the Minor Prophets at breakfast. If it is indeed true that I can still retain the ear of one who is earnestly desirous that the third man on the left should liberate the mustard I feel I ought not to withhold this gift from the public.

There is no religious movement to-day more important than the retreat movement, and I offer my little book respectfully to all who are seeking to promote it.

H. F. B. M.

CONTENTS

ST. CYPRIAN

"A bishop, blameless, the steward of God."—*Titus* i. 7.

I

I AM going to try to give you a glimpse of the character of St. Cyprian, Bishop of Carthage and Primate of the African Church, who was martyred in the year 257.

I shall say nothing on three subjects which are of great interest to historians and theologians—Cyprian's conception of, and development of, the Episcopal office, his share in the controversy about the rebaptism of heretics, and his rather stormy relations with the See of Rome. I am merely going to try to picture the man himself and his times and his faithful witness.

First, then, Carthage itself. You all know Turner's picture in the National Gallery of Dido building Carthage. Dido never saw such a Carthage as Turner imagined, but Cyprian did. The city itself was that sort of gorgeous vision of classical magnificence. Roman Africa was the strip along the north coast and it had two great gates into the awful unknown interior. One was Egypt, the other was Carthage. The province was not flat like Egypt, it was a splendid land of mountain and plateau. Fast vessels with a good wind covered the distance from Rome in two days. Once when Cato wished to frighten the Senate about the power of Carthage he suddenly held up a ripe fig and said, "That was picked in Carthage two days ago."

The Roman province of Carthage in Cyprian's day realized the dream our own Imperialists have for our overseas dominions. It was a magnificent piece of prosperous civilization. The city itself was amazingly picturesque. It clustered round a central rock three hundred feet high, a pyramid of steep streets, public buildings, palaces. Seaward lay the two harbours crowded with shipping, landward lay an immense suburb where the notables had their country seats each in splendid grounds. I suppose the Palaces of the Pashas and other wealthy Turks which line the Bosphorus are a modern parallel. Hills covered with shrines and villas encircled the scene, beyond lay the snows of the Atlas, and the whole was bathed in the splendid African light. And yet all the more thoughtful men had an instinctive knowledge that society was sick unto death. We have no conception of exactly such a state of things : however fallen a European state is, it knows what it must do to be saved. But the thoughtful men of A.D. 248 saw that human society and human nature were rotten and dying, and knew of no help or hope.

Cyprian was still a Pagan in middle life—he was the leading barrister and rhetorician of Carthage. Such a man had a position of influence in ancient society to which there is no exact parallel to-day. His power was more like the power of a modern newspaper. He was very wealthy, he had a beautiful country house on the outskirts of the city, he is supposed to describe it in one of his letters, its marble halls, its gilded ceilings, its frescoed walls, its exquisite gardens.

All that was best in the aristocracy of Carthage counted him a dear and honoured friend. He must have been extraordinarily attractive, very calm and equable, bright, sunny, and affectionate, with a great dignity and sweetness.

Such was the man who at the age of forty-seven was converted to the Catholic religion. It came about in this way. Deeply conscious of the sins of society it became clear to him that if the Empire was to hold together, it must preserve its religiousness. This led him to study the extraordinary body of people who refused to take part in the religious customs of the Empire. He was a candid and noble-minded critic. The wonderful power Christianity had over its devotees struck him. He looked deeper and found it preserved many Christians in perfect chastity—this he knew no power on earth could do. At the same time God set in his path an exquisite embodiment of the Faith in the old priest Cæcilian. In Cæcilian and those whom Cæcilian could show him, Cyprian recognized a Divine Power and Presence working moral miracles. He became a catechumen. It was the noblest catechumenate. He consecrated the whole of his mental training and eloquence to the service of the Catholic Religion. He gained grace before his baptism to become perfectly chaste in thought, word and deed. He gave all his property away in charity, parted with his country house and its lovely gardens, and went to live with Cæcilian. Cæcilian was old and failing, and his spiritual son nursed him in his sickness, and closed his eyes in death.

Cyprian was baptized at Easter, 246, and was ordained a deacon almost at once. For two years he lived as deacon and priest, and then when Donatus the Bishop died, the Christian multitude besieged Cyprian's lodging and elected him Bishop. He resisted, but the strength of the demand of the laity carried the day. It was very irregular and very extraordinary, and until almost the end of his life there was a small but strong opposition to him in the Church which treated him very much as some of the hereditary Roman Catholic clergy treated Cardinal Manning.

The Church would not allow Cyprian to live plainly and obscurely in a back street. It bought back his country house, refurnished him with means, and made the great Thascius Cyprianus resume his place in the society of Carthage—but now as Bishop. Of course, this made his life doubly hard and dangerous, but Cyprian saw that it was right, and for the first time a great and courted citizen of the Empire was also a Christian Bishop and Primate. Then almost at once the most appalling thing happened. The Empire was at the beginning of its death agonies ; on all sides its frontiers were threatened. The plague was sweeping over country after country and there was the possibility of a great famine. All the noblest men said, " We must return to a purer, nobler religion." So when an abundant harvest had removed the fear of famine, the whole Empire was required to join in a sacrifice of thanksgiving to the gods, and an edict was issued against any who should refuse. The Church of course refused, and appeared before the world as the enemy of religion and traitor to the Empire.

But there had been a thirty-eight years' peace for the Church ; even middle-aged men had never known a persecution ; softness and faithlessness had crept in : nearly half the Christians in Carthage apostatized, some out and out, others by evasion. Some of these bought from corrupt officials certificates of having sacrificed without actually sacrificing, others managed to slip past the altar, others dressed up heathen proxies to represent them, and there were heartrending cases of fathers dechristianizing themselves to save their wives and children.

On the other hand, the conduct of those who stood firm was magnificent, their enthusiasm was great. " Happy prison," they cried, " whose gloom is more brilliant than the sun itself."

At the outset of the persecution the Bishop had to decide with his Synod whether he should remain to die, or go into concealment and guide the Church through her difficulties. But there was really no doubt that it was his duty to live. Our Lord had ordered the Apostles to live as long as possible, and St. Paul in obedience fled from city to city. Cyprian knew it was his duty to do the same : twelve years afterwards he felt his work was done ; then he remained and died. For fourteen months the Archbishop ruled the Church from a secret place. Every day began with the Bishop's Eucharist, and was a day of vigorous administrative activity. The record of every martyr's death was sent to the Bishop that it might be put on the diptychs and calendared for the future. Never did a Church more greatly need guidance. When the brunt of the persecution was over the remorse of the lapsed was awful : some rushed back and purged their offence with martyrdom ; others remained in the churches day and night in an agony of

penitence.   Should they be restored to Communion ?
Some said not, that the Church on earth could not absolve
such sin.   Meanwhile the devotion to the martyrs and
confessors increased proportionately : they had saved
the Church.   Crowds visited them in prison.   Mass was
celebrated frequently in their cells, people kept vigils
of prayer that they might be arrested and so enabled
to wait on those who had been tortured.

So arose the hope that the merits of the confessors
atoned for the sin of the lapsed, and fallen Christians
gained letters from confessors pleading for their restoration.   This was really a big and new problem for the
Church to think out, and it was largely due to Cyprian's
calm statesmanship that it was solved wisely, and that
the authority of the priesthood was not usurped by the
authority of the confessors.   The priests were ordered
to administer penance to the lapsed, and then after a while,
with or without the petition of a confessor, to restore
them to communion.   When the persecution was over
the Bishop was able to return and rule the Church from
his beautiful home near Carthage.

Then came the plague.   I suppose the plague of the
third century was the most terrible visitation the world has
seen.   Just as peace and order were being restored to the
Church this universal horror and misery came.   It was a
kind of malignant typhoid, very rapid, and almost always
fatal.   The plague revealed heathen society to itself ; it
revealed its egotism.   People fled and left the dead and
dying in their houses, or they threw them into the street,
or they stabbed and poisoned them.   It was a mad reign
of terror in which every convention, every restraint not
based on strong principle, broke down.   It was the

Christian opportunity. Cyprian gathered the Church together, and, seating himself on the white linen-covered throne of the Pontiff, gave his motto for the time, " It behoves us to behave comformably with our noble lineage," and formed a scheme for the systematic care of the city. Practically the whole Christian community organized itself, raised large funds, formed a nursing and a burying staff, and worked day and night rescuing from the hell of the streets and houses those who a year or two before had shrieked, " The Christians to the lions!" There let us leave Bishop Cyprian for the moment, sitting on his white linen-draped throne in the heart of the plague ; his faithful people, the feet and hands with which he succoured from madness, despair, and death the fellow citizens who regarded them as the enemies of all religion.

We leave him with two reflections. The first is this : Here is a perfect illustration of what is meant by conversion. This noble-thinking, noble-speaking, noble-living Pagan is so impressed by the life of Christ as it reappears in His followers that he desires to imitate it, and in response to prayer and effort receives the gift of Faith. And when he has received the gift of Faith he finds himself in touch with the spiritual world and an unseen order, taking human nature by a divine path to a divine end. So he puts his whole being completely at the service of our Lord—he does what the rich young man in the Gospel would not do ; he preserves himself in spotless chastity, gives all his goods to the poor, and his trained intellect to the Catholic Religion. It is St. John over again—the man who begins with a complete oblation of his will, and is therefore at once Israel, a

Prince of God ; how gloriously a Prince of God is shown, I think, by his whole attitude towards martyrdom. It was only a perfectly disciplined selfless man who could decide not to be martyred when half the Church was apostatizing, who from his retreat could inspire the confessors to the noblest constancy, and who afterwards, when his people who had grown to love him passionately were entreating him to conceal himself, could say, " No, now I feel that I shall serve God best by staying and dying," and who so stayed and died.

The second reflection is this : It was the conduct of Cyprian and his people in the plague which began to explain Christianity to the pagans. Zeal for the Faith even unto death was a great inspiration to the Church, but the world thought it criminal obstinacy. It was the love of the Church for all mankind, whom it now saw from its Maker's standpoint which converted the world. Let that be our lesson. It is a glorious act to uphold the Faith even unto death, but that separates us from the world ; it does not unite us to it. The world does not know the language of the Faith, but it understands the language of Charity. We must translate the Faith into terms of Charity if we would convince men.

II

You will never see the glory of the Christian stand against the religious decrees of the Empire until you realize that the decrees themselves were eminently reasonable. When I read a leading article in *The Times* on an ecclesiastical question I am moved to reflect how greatly the writer would have disliked the Church of the first three centuries ; indeed, I greatly wish we could have persuaded Mr. Gilbert Chesterton to write a history of the early Church from the standpoint of *The Times*. And this is by no means to disparage the personal character of the gentlemen who write the leading articles on ecclesiastical matters for *The Times*.

Consider the situation. Valerian the Emperor and Macrian his chancellor, who enforced the decrees against the Christians in 257 and 258, were among the noblest men of any age. The barbarians, to use Archbishop Benson's phrase, had girt the empire with an ever-contracting ring of fire. At any moment they might be anywhere, while the plague was everywhere. The essence of the Empire was unity symbolized by the adoration of the Emperor's Majesty, and yet within the Empire was an ever-increasing multitude who refused to perform the sacred act which was the bond of the unity. You must remember that to the inhabitants of the Empire what was anti-Roman seemed to be anti-human, and that the Christian assembly was really believed to be the scene of devilish rites. In every district there was a local chief of these Christians, and a mysterious organization from which anyone who obeyed the law of sacrificing to the majesty of Augustus was cast out. This organization haunted the cemeteries ; and the tombs of those who had been executed for disobedience to the state were objects of extraordinary devotion to its members.

And so now, when the plague was partly abated, another tremendous effort was made to deal with these dangerous people. Their chiefs were to be banished, their meetings suppressed, and their visits to the cemeteries forbidden. You observe, then, that three points of Christian doctrine and practice were so conspicuous that even the heathen state recognized them and singled them out for attack. These three points were the Apostolic succession of the Bishops, the Eucharist, and active relations with the faithful departed in a reciprocity of prayer.

The struggle at Carthage began on the 30th August, 257, when the Proconsul sent for the Bishop. He was a city magnate as well as a Christian Bishop, and he was examined in the Proconsul's sanctum.

" The Emperors have done me the honour to send me a despatch in which they direct the people who do not follow the Roman religion to conform to the Roman ceremonies. I have in consequence made enquiries about your position. What have you to say about it ? "

" I am a Christian and a Bishop. I know no other God but the one and true God who made heaven and earth, the sea and all that is therein. He is the God we Christians serve, and we pray to him night and day for ourselves and for all men and for the safety of the Emperors themselves."

" You intend to persist in this ? "

" No other course is possible."

" Well, then, will it be possible for you to take your departure as an exile to the city of Curubis ? "

" I depart."

Cyprian was allowed time to order his affairs, and on September 14th he arrived at the little town on the coast fifty miles off, to which he had been banished.

That night he dreamt. He dreamt that he was standing before the Proconsul, and that the Proconsul was writing his final sentence on a tablet. Cyprian could not see what he was writing, but behind the Proconsul stood a tall and very splendid young man, and the young man was looking over the Proconsul's shoulder and reading what he had written on the tablet. Presently he looked up and his eye caught Cyprian's. He did not speak, but he made a gesture which Cyprian understood. Cyprian knew that he was to be beheaded. "May I have a day to prepare?" he asked with keen anxiety. The young man looked down again, then again he looked at Cyprian and made a gesture of assent. This was a great joy to Cyprian. He recognized that he was now to die, and so did all his attendants—they always spoke quite naturally and cheerfully on the death day which was coming as "the morrow," and it is a remarkable fact that the martyrdom occurred on the anniversary of the day on which Cyprian dreamed the dream.

The year passed in Eucharist and prayer, and a ministry through agents to the clergy of local social status who had been sent to the mines. In the dark and awful heat they lived, stifled with the smoke of the smelting furnaces, half-starved and half-naked, sleeping on the bare ground. They suffered greatly from not being able to offer the Holy Sacrifice, but the Archbishop consoled them by reminding them that in their own persons they were now God's holy and immaculate victims. At the end of the first year came a fresh edict : the first had utterly failed. It is now believed that it was the magnificent translation of the bodies of St. Peter and St. Paul at Rome which demonstrated the failure of the first edict and evoked the second. The second rescript was very thorough—

death for the clergy, confiscation and slavery for the laity.

The moment Cyprian heard of it he came back to Carthage. There was no fear of apostasy now—all the clergy were at their posts, the laity, all strong, silent, quiet, and as the Archbishop from his linen-covered throne had given the motto in the plague, so he gave one now for the passion of the Church, " Not death, death-lessness ; no dread, only gladness."

As soon as the rescript arrived, Galerius the Proconsul, who was ill at Utica, told Cyprian to go to his country house and wait a summons there. He went, and was besieged by the faithful imploring him to fly ; even great pagan magnates begged him to let them provide for his safety. Cyprian smiled serenely and refused. Meanwhile, the Proconsul grew worse, and he sent for Cyprian to Utica. But Cyprian determined to die at Carthage among his people ; so when the officers arrived the Archbishop had disappeared, leaving a message that when the Proconsul came to Carthage he would appear before him. This spurred the Proconsul to action ; wretchedly ill as he was, he travelled to Carthage, and the night he arrived at the villa of Sextus, where he was to stay, the Bishop, who knew all about his movements, was back at the Thascian Gardens. At daybreak on September 13th the Gardens were surrounded by a cordon of soldiers, and two high officers drove up to the Hall in a chariot, the Proconsul's aide-de-camp and the deputy governor of the prison. Bishop Cyprian came out of his house with eager step and masterful look, and took his place between them—he was extraordinarily like the Blessed Thomas More in his bearing—and the chariot drove away to the Villa of Sextus. When they got there the Proconsul was too ill to see Cyprian, and so it was that he was remanded till the morrow as had been forewarned in the dream. He was treated with the most distinguished courtesy, the mansion of the first *princeps* of the city was placed at his disposal, and supper was prepared for an immense party of guests. The Bishop spent the day in ordering the affairs of the Church. At nightfall his ecclesiastical household and all the leading Christians supped with Bishop Cyprian at the mansion of the *princeps*. Meanwhile, the approaches were blocked by an enormous silent crowd. The whole Church of Carthage surrounded the house to keep the vigil of the Bishop's last night on earth ; behind the Christians stood crowds of pagans sorrowing for the death of the great citizen. In the course of the evening Cyprian sent out a message to the Christian crowd that the young Christian women should be carefully protected.

It certainly looks as though these people, keeping the all-night vigil, had a clearer perception of the spiritual realities than members of the Church of England have to-day. Before the Catholic revival the last group of people who showed that spirit were John Evelyn and his friends going up to the altar for Communion under the loaded muskets of the Puritans. Most of their successors went out of the Church of England as non-jurors, and there were few again until the time of Newman, but among the few was Dr. Johnson. He is the only Anglican of his time whom I can imagine as keeping an all-night vigil with a martyr before his death, and that is because Dr. Johnson's religion was the religion of the

Church of Carthage. To him, as to the Church of
Carthage, the three great facts which the heathen
assaulted under the names of the assemblies, the chiefs
and the cemeteries, that is to say, the Eucharist, the
Apostolic Succession and the Communion of Saints,
were among the central verities. Yes, if you would
witness before the world as the Church of Cyprian
witnessed, if you would imitate its attitude and its acts,
then you must stand as that Church stood towards
the Eucharist, the hierarchy, the saints and the departed.

The 14th September was a gorgeous day, with cloud-
less sky and blazing sun. Cyprian started for the Sistine
Villa in the centre of a large group of officers surrounded
by a strong guard, followed by the greater part of the
population of the city. His biographer has sketched
the moment when he passed out of the dark cool streets
into the blazing plain where the stubble lay bare and the
vines stripped.

The Proconsul, who was really dying, was again too
ill to receive Cyprian at first, and he was taken to a quiet
shady room to wait. The chair given to him happened
to be covered with white linen. The Christians smiled,
for its covering made it a bishop's throne. The walk
had been intensely hot, and the thin robes of the Archbishop were soaked with perspiration, and as he sat still
in the gloom of the shuttered room an officer came to
him and nervously begged him to accept a change of
clothes. He wished himself to keep the clothes the
Archbishop was wearing. The man was a lapsed
Christian. God alone knows what his motive was.
Cyprian smilingly refused. " That," he said, " would

22

be to remedy a complaint which will probably be never felt again after to-day."

At the same instant he was summoned into the court. Galerius, ghastly, panting, dying, sat in his council for the last time, around him the magistrates of the city, behind him the six lictors with rods and axes, before him a chafing dish, the charcoal smouldering, and a box of incense. The trial lasted about twenty minutes. Galerius with great difficulty made a short speech, and explained that Cyprian was to suffer on the ground that he was a Bishop of the new spreading union which was in antagonism to the gods of the Roman unity. A clerk handed him a tablet and he read : " Our pleasure is that Thascius Cyprianus be executed with the sword."

" Thanks be to God," said the Archbishop.

The inner circle of Cyprian's friends felt an awful and solemn exultation : to them it meant God bestowing a martyr's crown. But the poor and simple could not rise so high, and they cried an exceeding bitter cry, " Let us also be beheaded with him." The guard closed round and led the way to a great level space in the park, surrounded by steep high slopes covered with trees. The multitude packed the great meadow and climbed up into the trees all round it, covering the ground and loading the trees with the brilliant colour of their dresses.

In the centre the legionaries made a great empty square, and into it walked St. Cyprian with his assistant priest, two deacons and a sub-deacon. There was an awful stillness. The Bishop unfastened his shoulder clasps and took off his big white cape, then he knelt, and spreading out his arms prostrated himself on the ground in prayer. After a time he rose and stood thinking ; he had always expected a revelation from God at the moment of death, but searching his mind he could not be clear that any of the thoughts there were not his own, so with splendid self-control and simplicity he was perfectly silent. He took off his dalmatic and gave it to his Deacons to hold. There was a delay. The executioner had not arrived. At last he came. "Give him twenty-five pounds," said Cyprian to his friends. Handkerchiefs were now rained on the ground all round the Bishop, and these the deacons spread out carefully so that the grass was covered with white linen to receive the precious relics of the Martyr's blood. He took a handkerchief, folded it, and began to bandage his own eyes, but he could not tie the knot behind easily, so the priest and one of the deacons tied it while Cyprian held it before his eyes. He knelt, bent his head to the blow, and then the executioner collapsed—it was an anxious moment for the Roman officers, they did not yet know the temper of the Christian crowd sufficiently well to understand that there would be no rescue. The Centurion himself took the sword—and dealing one blow of preternatural force, himself sent the spirit of Cyprian to the throne of God.

All day long the body of the Martyr lay where it had fallen, while enormous crowds, Christian and Pagan, defiled past in silence. With night came the burial. Carrying countless wax lights and torches, the Faithful, with prayer and great triumph, bore the Martyr to the cemetery and spent the long vigil at his tomb. And so, in the lovely light of dawn, they laid down their spent torches and went to their homes, feeling that his triumph was theirs also.

ST. JEROME

I

It may be remembered that in October, 1913, we kept the sixteenth centenary of the publication of the Edict of Milan by the Emperors Constantine and Licinius. This was the edict which decreed toleration for the Christian religion. It was issued in 313, and from that moment the Christianization of the Empire proceeded apace. Constantine remained the patron of Christianity, but he was not baptized until he was on his deathbed. He died in 337, and about 346 Jerome was born.

There were at that time two emperors. Constans ruled the Western Empire, making Milan his capital, and Constantius ruled the East, from Constantinople. The Arian controversy was still dividing Christians : the controversy as to whether our Lord is Eternal God or had been originated. The West was mostly free from it, but it was predominant in the East, and during Jerome's early boyhood, after the Western Emperor's death, the Arian Constantius was trying to impose his creed upon western Christians. Constantius was followed by Julian the Apostate, but Julian had died in the Persian campaign, and the Church had triumphed finally under Jovian, his successor, before Jerome, at the age of seventeen, was sent with his friend Bonosus to complete his education in Rome.

He was born, and up to this time had lived, at Stridon, a suburb, a sort of Chislehurst, of Aquileia, the ancestress of Venice, which lay to the north-east of where Venice now lies—between the Alps and the Adriatic. He came, apparently, of a hardy Dalmatian stock. His parents were Christians, but, as was the case with a great many at that time, Jerome was not baptized in infancy. Apparently they were moderately wealthy people, the sort of people who to-day would have a small place, a couple of cars, and men-servants ; but the boy saw life on a bigger scale, for he had the run of the house and park owned by the parents of his bosom friend Bonosus. A writer, who lived a little later, has described the country house life of these days—the early luncheon and the late dinner, the lawn tennis, the hunting, the riding, the swimming ; the big hall, where the family mostly lived, the mistress's sitting-room, the master's library, the winter dining-room, blackened with the smoke of the wood fires, for there was no chimney ; the summer dining-room, opening on the broad terrace. Jerome was familiar with all this. He was carefully educated by a tutor, but he says he was idle, and preferred the society of the stable boys ; he was very clever and restless, and he imbibed knowledge very easily.

Rome, in 363, was just at the supreme moment of its extent and architectural—I will not say magnificence, for it was a blatant, vulgar place—but prodigality. The whole series of buildings—temples, basilicas, palaces, forums, colonnades, arches, theatres and baths, studded with statues and relieved by gardens—the whole thing was still untouched by spoiler or decay. But for a hundred years it had ceased to be the seat of Empire, for Diocletian had reorganized the State, and the Emperors of the new *régime* found it advisable to keep clear of the conservative traditions of Rome and the rivalry of the patrician houses. If Napoleon III had rebuilt Lyons instead of Paris, and left Paris to the ancient nobility, you would have had a somewhat parallel situation.

Observe the effect of this on Rome : the Senate, although now only municipal in its functions, retained its state and a great deal of its prestige, while the patrician houses, which were wealthy almost beyond imagination, gave themselves semi-regal airs, and achieved an exquisiteness of manners and of luxury, which looked down with disdain on the coarser splendour of the far-away imperial court. It was as a part of their disdainful and exquisite conservatism that the men of the nobler families continued to give their adherence to the ancient national religion. They were pagans for the same reason that so many of our ancient families are Low Church.

It was an interesting and curious moment in the history of religion—the Emperor and the officials were more or less Christians; the Church was exceedingly strong and growing very wealthy ; the Bishop of Rome was an enormously wealthy and a very influential person. Christian priests and ecclesiastical personages swarmed all over Rome. Throughout the country, what religion there was was increasingly Christian ; the temples were disused, the pagan priesthood was disappearing in all country places ; but not so in Rome. In Rome many temples were disused, were covered with dirt and cobwebs, and showing signs of disrepair ; and there were many splendid churches, but the vast majority of the temples were fully staffed. The nobles and the Senate were disdainfully, defiantly pagan ; large subsidies were still given to the pagan priesthood, and all the solemnities of the pagan year were scrupulously observed. On the other hand, the majority of the ladies of the nobler families were Christians. Roman social custom gave immense power and independence to ladies at this time ; there was little attempt to coerce them in the matter of religion. The pagan religion had become an ancestral tradition and a political asset ; there was nothing but Christianity for those who desired a strong, spiritual religion, and the religion of some of the great Roman ladies was one of the strongest forces of the time. I shall have a good deal to say about that presently.

Those of you who have been to Rome can have no difficulty in making a mental picture of the forums and temples of the city into which young Jerome and young Bonosus came as students ; but you must remember to put in what has completely disappeared—the domestic houses, tall, steeply gabled, built of brick, with overhanging balconies, lining narrow winding streets and making deep shadows ; you must put in the dense jostling crowd, all the pavements as full during the hours of promenade as the pavement in front of Peter Robinson's ; you must imagine the brilliant mantles of the gentlemen, the picturesque dirtiness of the poorer people, the ladies painted and dressed as if for the ballet, and carried along in ivory litters.

Jerome and Bonosus had hired a little room in one of the very tall houses, and here they ensconced themselves, no doubt bewildered and home-sick, high above the city's roar. Student life in Rome in those days was more like student life in Heidelberg or in Edinburgh than University life in Oxford (for a parallel to Oxford you must go further back, to student life in Greece). Jerome worked very hard at literature, Latin and Greek, and at rhetoric—rhetoric is the art of making oneself effective as a thinker and speaker. He studied all the best speakers of the day, and he got the reputation of a brilliant boy. It was now that he began to collect a library—a library which grew and grew, and which he carried about with him wherever he went. He must have been a lean, dark, vivid boy, impetuous, hot-tempered and attractive. He was under no moral discipline, he had to take care of himself, and for a time he failed, he fell into sin ; he did not fall into great excess, but he had never been baptized, and his life was not conspicuously better than that of his companions. But there was always a religious side to his character, and he was immensely impressed by the catacombs. The catacombs had become a show place after the close of the persecutions. Thither, on Sunday afternoons, went streams of citizens to wander through the dark corridors and gape reverently at the tombs of the martyrs. (The Archdeacon Damasus had done his best to develop an enthusiasm for the martyrs, and had written beautiful inscriptions of honour for the tombs of the early bishops.) Next time you go to the catacombs do not forget the dark-haired boy who was drawn back to them time after time, and there began to see the glory of curbing his passions and giving himself to Christ ; the boy to whom you owe your knowledge of the Bible.

In the middle of this student time occurred the Christian riots over the election to the Bishopric. Damasus and his party were in the right, but it was a sorry business. I doubt whether the bloodshed disgusted Jerome with the Church. At any rate here was a living cause, a cause in which men were ready to die, and Jerome already saw that there was no cause nobler than the Christian. He was not a pagan, remember ; he was an unattached Christian, and except for the fact that they have been baptized in infancy the majority of young Englishmen are very much what Jerome was at that point.

When his three years at the University were over, Jerome spent some time in Gaul, chiefly at Treves, then the seat of the Imperial Court. Apparently he went there with a view to practising as an advocate, but one of the accidents which are providential turned his thoughts another way. Rufinus, a young gentleman of Aquileia, had become a great friend of Jerome's, and when he heard that Jerome was going to Gaul he asked him to try to procure for him a copy of St. Hilary's Commentary on the Psalms and his book on the Councils. Jerome made the copy himself, and St. Hilary's Commentary raised in him the passion for Biblical study which became the main preoccupation of his life. Henceforward all his interests were exclusively Christian. He was baptized in Rome, and you must remember what that meant; it meant submitting to a severe and prolonged discipline; it meant the radical cure of vicious tendencies; it meant the heart-whole acceptance of the Christian creed by one of the acutest minds of the time, the heart-whole devotion of a passionate and impetuous nature to the cause of Christ and the Church.

Indeed, once in the heart of the Christian Church, the recipient of her sacraments, young Jerome felt himself called to the most complete expression of Christian self-sacrifice that age knew. To become a Christian inevitably in Jerome's case meant becoming, to some extent or other, an ascetic.

Recall the picture of Rome I drew just now and remember that at that time, in the awful deserts of Egypt, there were twenty thousand men and nearly thirty thousand women living the lives of solitaries either in organized clusters or in scattered independence. It was the protest of the Christian spirit against the intolerable trammels of a most elaborate pagan civilization which it was powerless to banish from the cities. To fight it the Christian spirit had to retire into the desert and array itself against it in utter self-immolation.

It was in 341, a quarter of a century before this time, that Athanasius fleeing from persecution had come to Rome attended by two hermits of the Nitrian desert who had left their solitude to accompany him into exile. They had described and preached the ascetic life—and they moved the noblest Christians among the noble Christian ladies to the depths of their being. In many respects the position of these ladies was an intolerable one. Maintaining their place in general society involved days entirely occupied with the apparatus of living luxuriously ; the bath, the toilet, and the banquet—disfigured in all the great houses by the introduction of disgraceful dances between the courses—consumed their lives. And such a toilet ! quite literally these Christian ladies were all dressed like the transformation ballet in a pantomime: powder, paint and golden wigs decorated their faces and heads, and their semi-transparent draperies were so heavily weighted with gold and gems that they

used to totter to their couches supported by their
slaves. There had seemed no avoiding all this : but the
influence of Athanasius and the hermits raised a
revolt. The sleek, comfortable clergy of Rome were
almost as much horrified as the pagan patricians, for
now one great matron after another laid aside her
trappings and assumed the ascetic dress. The Lady
Marcella retired to her villa in the Campagna and took
the house for a hermitage, and the gardens for a wilderness. The Lady Sophronia arranged a little cell in her
city mansion and lived in it. Then Marcella came back
to the city and turned the whole of her vast palace on
the Aventine into a lay convent. Indeed it exactly
realized Bunyan's House Beautiful. It became the
centre of a group of devout ladies, some quite retired,
some partially, some still in the world, but all united in
finding a haven of purity and peace in the palace on the
Aventine. Among these, still painted and jewelled,
still tottering between her slaves, was one who was to
become in time the greatest of them all, the Lady Paula,
descendant of the Scipios and the Gracchi and the
ancient kings of Sparta. Paula, and by her side her young
daughter, the naturally saintly, the heavenly-minded
Eustochium.

We are not surprised that the young Jerome flew into
this society like a bird to its nest. Very soon his im-
petuosity landed him in a scrape with the larger world.
Melania was a young Spanish lady who at twenty-three
had lost her husband and two of her three children.
She had imbibed the ascetic spirit, and when they died
she stretched out her arms to a figure of our Lord and said,
" Now, my Lord, I am free to serve Thee." She was of

the highest aristocracy and very wealthy. She left everything, even her one remaining child, and sailed to Egypt to join the solitaries.

Jerome warmly applauded and helped her, and some of the furious indignation which the incident aroused in Roman society was levelled against him, but I imagine this caused him very little concern.

About this time he returned to Aquileia and set about living the ascetic life in grim earnest with a group of kindred spirits. The lads made various attempts; one went into a cave in the Alps, Bonosus to an island off the coast, Jerome and Paulinian, his brother, tried to do the hardest thing of all: they went back to the old home at Stridon and tried to be ascetics there. But they found it impossible. The old Bishop of the diocese objected to these extreme practices of Jerome and Paulinian, and Jerome lost his temper with him, and said in public the sort of things which it is very improper for an extreme young layman to say about a respectable moderate Bishop. After relieving his mind in this naughty manner, Jerome went off into a solitary place in the country and tried to be a hermit there, but he did not persevere for very long. It was like an inhabitant of Brighton trying to be a hermit in a wood on the slope of the South Downs. Before long Jerome and Paulinian were back in Aquileia, and there they met all the other boys who had failed too.

But—and this is where the saint begins to emerge in Jerome and his friends—because they had failed in this first attempt they did not give up the idea. We must go to the East, they said, and visit the great schools of the ascetic life. At this juncture it happened by one of the accidents which are of God's decree, that a Syrian priest passed through Aquileia on his way back from Rome, and he invited the young men to travel to Syria with him. They did so, and after making the acquaintance of the great St. Basil, Bishop of Cæsarea, on the way, they reached the Syrian Antioch at the close of the year 373.

The chief feature of Antioch always impresses my imagination: an immensely broad street, four miles long, with a double roofed-in marble colonnade on both sides, open to the sky only down the middle of the street. Imagine the beauty of the groupings in that street in the black shadows cut by brilliant sunshine.

Rome was Pagan so far as the official class was concerned, Antioch was Christian, and exhibited all the Eastern enthusiasm for the subtleties of theology. It was torn at this time by a tremendous schism. There was an Arian Bishop Euzoius and an orthodox Bishop in communion with the rest of the East of moderate temper, Meletius, so moderate that some Arians had concurred in his election, and another orthodox Bishop, Paulinus, supported by the extremely orthodox, who had obtained the recognition of Rome and the West for him, and who were maintaining him in opposition to Meletius on the score that the concurrence of Arians had vitiated Meletius' election. Jerome's friend and courier was of the party of Paulinus, so Jerome was on that side too. Indeed as a Western he would naturally have sided with the man the West recognized. But at this time he did not mix himself up in the controversy. He felt he must take advantage of the theological stimulus which Antioch provided to study, and he became absorbed in the interests aroused by the teaching of Apollinaris, Bishop of Laodicea, who was head of the theological school, a great scholar and controversialist, afterwards known as a great heretic. But another providential accident brought this agreeable life to a close. One day Evagrius, the friend and pilot of Jerome, took him to visit an old solitary, who lived in a lonely spot about thirty miles away.

The story of this old man is a beautiful one, and it played a great part in the life of St. Jerome. Malchus had been a merchant who had been captured by a tribe of Bedaween while travelling with his caravan. They took him off as a slave into the depths of the desert and made him a herdsman. One day in the agony of his misery and loneliness he broke down and loudly called on God to take his life. Presently a gentle voice reached him in his distress. It was the voice of a woman, his companion in slavery. She spoke to him of the love of God, and she saved him and restored him to patience and hope. They talked to each other about religious experience after this. They knew of the solitaries, and they made a grand resolution to regard their servitude as being a form of the hermit's life. In this way they persevered, and at last a way to escape opened. They escaped together, but neither returned to the world; she entered a convent, and he went to a wild spot and there lived the life of a solitary in the accustomed way.

This supremely noble story touched Jerome to the heart. He could restrain himself no longer, he flung his books aside, persuaded his youthful friends once more, and all with one exception went off to a monastery on the edge of the desert of Chalcis. At the monastery they were all stricken with severe illness, two of them died, Jerome nearly died; but he did not return to the world on his recovery, he went off alone into the desert and embraced the full hardship of the hermit's life. From the desert he writes to Heliodorus the friend who had left the party and gone back to Aquileia, and sings the praises of the hermit's life :

" O desert blooming with the flowers of Christ !

" O wilderness where are shaped the stones of which the city of the great King is built !

" O solitude where men converse familiarly with God !

" What are you doing among the worldly, O Heliodorus, you who are greater than all the world ?

" How long shall the cover of roofs weigh you down, how long shall the prison of the smoking city confine you ?

" Do you fear poverty ? But Christ calls the poor blessed.

" Are you frightened at the prospect of labour ? But no athlete is crowned without sweat.

" Are you thinking about daily food ? But faith fears not hunger.

" Do you dread to lay your fasting body on the bare ground ? But Christ lies beside you.

" Do the tangled locks of a neglected toilet shock you ? But your head is Christ. You are too luxurious, my brother, if you wish both to enjoy yourself here with the world and afterwards to reign with Christ."

Yes, but his description of its spiritual joys is only one side of the hermit's life : he sketches another in a letter addressed to the young lady, Eustochium, Paula's daughter, and one of the most spiritual of the devout ladies of Rome. This letter was written later—it has some of the eloquence of retrospect about it :

" I sat alone because my soul was black with bitterness.

" My shapeless limbs were clad in a frightful sack, my squalid skin had taken the colour of an Ethiopian's flesh.

" I spent whole days shedding tears and breathing sighs, and when in spite of myself I was overcome with sleep, I let fall upon the naked earth a body so emaciated that the bones scarce held together."

All this, he says, so far from conquering his earthly passions seemed to rouse them. " Thus destitute of all help I cast myself at the feet of Jesus, I bathed them with my tears, I wiped them with my hair, I often passed the night and the day in crying and beating my breast and ceased not till God making Himself heard, peace came back to me.

" God is my witness that sometimes, after having for a long time lifted up my eyes to heaven, I believed myself transported into the midst of the choirs of angels and filled with confidence and joy I sang, ' We will run after Thee for the odour of Thy perfumes '."

You will be amused after reading these two letters to learn that Jerome had brought his library with him into the desert and housed it carefully, that scribes came and camped with him and copied letters or wrote at his dictation, that monks and hermits came and talked with him and that he kept up a vigorous correspondence with his friends. He maintained himself. He culti-vated vegetables and he copied books and made rush baskets.

He was a layman, remember, and he must have been communicated occasionally with the reserved Sacrament

He was a fine scholar with a scholar's love of style, and his recreation consisted in reading the best pagan authors. He came to think this to be wrong. He had a vision of the Judgment. " Who art thou ? " asked the Judge. " I am a Christian," replied Jerome. " Thou liest," said the Judge, " thou art a Ciceronian, for where thy treasure is there is thy heart also."

Jerome abandoned Cicero after this, and the scruple had enormous consequences. He determined to learn Hebrew as a penance. There happened to be a converted Jew in a monastery near by, who became Jerome's tutor. Jerome hated the task. He detested Hebrew, and nothing but his ascetic vocation made him persevere. So you see that it was directly out of his asceticism that his power came to give the Bible in an adequate shape to the Christian Church.

It was the increasing vehemence of the controversies of the Syrian Church which ultimately drove Jerome out of the desert, where theological controversy ran high among the monks and hermits. To the three parties of Euzoius, Meletius and Paulinus, two more were added in the course of the three years. Meletius and Paulinus agreed that whichever of the two survived should succeed the other, and the most distinguished of the followers of Meletius concurred in this, but the other Syrian Bishops declined at any price to have Paulinus Bishop of Antioch and their ecclesiastical superior. This divided the friends of Meletius. Meanwhile Apollinaris, the brilliant Bishop of Laodicea, had begun to champion a new theory about the union of our Lord's two natures which destroyed our Lord's perfect humanity, as the Arian theory would destroy his deity. The Apollinarians separated themselves from the other Christians of Antioch and got a Bishop of their own, so now there were five parties in Antioch quarrelling over four Bishops.

Jerome, as a friend of Paulinus, the Bishop who had the sympathies of Rome, found himself an object of suspicion to his neighbours in the desert who were all sympathisers with Meletius. He returned to Antioch and went on with his studies there. He was naturally drawn closer to Bishop Paulinus in whose cause he had suffered some social obloquy, and Paulinus pressed, in fact forced, the Priesthood upon him.

The action of forcing Holy Orders on unwilling candidates is one of the most inexplicable features in the feeling and conduct of early times. Jerome told the Bishop plainly that if he hoped to wean him from the ascetic life by making him a Priest he was mistaken. He submitted to ordination, but it is said that never under any circumstances did he say Mass or act as a Priest in any way. It was his association with Paulinus which, probably against his will, brought St. Jerome at this point to Constantinople, where he spent three years in the heart of the whirlpool of the ecclesiastical troubles of the time.

This story of Jerome is a story of the most extraordinary contrasts of environments. From the desert of Chalcis to Constantinople ! The world presents no such contrasts now, for no city has the brilliant, feverish, exuberant life of the New Rome of those times.

To-day, when you have crossed the Sea of Marmora, there will rise out of the opalescent water a vision of pearl-white domes and minarets which, as seen from the sea, is more like the New Jerusalem than any other city in the world, and less like it than any other city, I suppose, when one gets inside it. Constantine built his city on the seven low hills of a triangular spur of land which is bounded by the Sea of Marmora on the South, the Straits of the Bosphorus on the East, and the narrow winding creek called the Golden Horn which penetrates Europe from the Bosphorus on the North. It was all built to order and must have been very spick and span and uninteresting but very magnificent. In addition to the usual grandiose public buildings there were five thousand mansions in gardens, like Dorchester House and Bridgwater House. The city too, like all the later Roman cities, was decorated with marbles filched from Greece and elsewhere.

The year before Jerome went to Constantinople the fortune of the Church there had changed for the better. For forty years the See had been held by Arians under a succession of Arian Emperors. Now a Catholic Emperor, Theodosius, had come to the throne.

Basil of Cæsarea in Cappadocia, the second of the Greek Fathers, had been leader of the Catholics in the East. He died just as this great opportunity of realizing his hopes dawned, but left behind him an Elisha in Gregory Nazianzen, the third of the Greek Fathers, and now the little band of Catholics in Arian Constantinople begged Gregory to come and take charge of them and prepare them for the task of reasserting the Catholic position there.

Gregory, by nature very retiring and gentle, felt the call to go. When Jerome reached Constantinople he found Gregory presiding over the little Catholic congregation in a private house, and he joined himself to him and always speaks of him with gratitude and affection.

Next year, in 380, the Emperor came to Constantinople and there was a great setting to rights. The Arians were bundled out and the people forced Gregory into the throne. It was another illustration of this strange raising people to dignity by force. The Emperor summoned a Council to meet and compose the troubles of the Church, but they became worse before the Council met. The Church of Alexandria grew jealous of the prospective power of the Church of Constantinople and there followed that astounding incident worthy of a Sherlock Holmes story, " The Adventure of the Egyptian Corn Ships." The Alexandrians sent a party of Bishops to Constantinople with the autumn fleet which brought corn to the capital. They broke into the principal church in the middle of the night, consecrated a man called Maximus whom they had brought with them, and enthroned him as Bishop of Constantinople.

In May, 381, the Council of Constantinople, whose extension of the Nicene Creed we use, assembled. Meletius, Bishop of Antioch, presided : the Council recognized his right to his See and declared the arrangement he had made with Paulinus null and void. Directly after, Meletius died and Gregory, Bishop of Constantinople, became President. Then came Timothy, the new Bishop of Alexandria—the See had been vacant when the Council was summoned—with a party of followers championing Maximus against Gregory. The Council rejected Maximus, and to make matters easier Gregory resigned, and the Bishops asked the Emperor to nominate a Bishop. The Emperor nominated an unbaptized noble, a catechumen of the Church. Nectarius was baptized, consecrated and enthroned at once, and took his seat as

President of the Second General Council, wearing his
Bishop's insignia over the white robes of the newly
baptized.

Before the Council ended, a deputation of Western Bishops arrived proposing a similar Council for similar purposes at Rome the next year. The Eastern Bishops and
Theodosius were very angry with the Western Bishops
and Gratian. This Western movement was an assertion
of the pre-eminence of the Roman See drawn forth by
the same fear of Constantinople which had led Alexandria to behave so badly, and it is thought St. Ambrose
had a good deal to do with it. In the end two Eastern
Bishops went to the Roman Council, Paulinus of Antioch
whom Constantinople would not recognize and who had
always been a favourite with the West, and his friend
Epiphanius, Archbishop of Salamis, whose special reason
for going was to expose the Apollinarian heresy. Jerome
agreed to go with Paulinus to Rome. Jerome is almost
entirely silent about his time in Constantinople, and he
never openly mentions the Second Œcumenical Council.

Pause to notice the situation. Here are four of the
eight Fathers of the Church at the most critical moment
in her history somewhat at loggerheads in the matter of
authority ; on the one side St. Ambrose and St. Jerome
and on the other St. Basil and St. Gregory Nazianzen.
But a schism between East and West was averted; the
Roman Council accepted most of the decisions of the
Council of Constantinople when it came to examine
them and it sank ultimately into a position of no importance, while the Council of Constantinople became
recognized as the Second Œcumenical Council.

In our story, though, the Roman Council plays an

important part. The Fathers of the Council were honoured by the patricians of Rome, and St. Jerome was received again with joy in the House Beautiful, the Palace of the Lady Marcella on the Aventine. I imagine that it was through the influence of the great ladies that Jerome was given the important post of Secretary to the Council. This brought him under the notice of Pope Damasus, and it is on his friendship with Pope Damasus that the rest of our story turns.

When the Council was over Pope Damasus retained Jerome by his side as Secretary of the Roman See. He became an early predecessor of Cardinal Gasparri, and it is for this reason that he appears, wherever he is represented in Art, wearing the robes and hat of a Cardinal, because since mediæval times a Cardinal has always held this office.

The word Cardinalis is probably used for an ecclesiastic in the sense of Principal, and it survives in this sense at Rome, where the Priests chosen to be the Pope's Council are made incumbents of the principal Churches and are therefore Cardinals; and also in our own St. Paul's, where the two principal Priests among the Minor Canons are Senior and Junior Cardinal.

For three years Jerome transacted a good deal of the business of the diocese of Rome, and all the time he steadily prosecuted his studies. He was a marvel of diligence. The Bishop had considerable literary ability himself and he was a very able and forcible person : in Jerome he had found the man capable of doing what he wanted done, a revision of the Latin versions of the Gospels.

43

As you know, the Christian Church in Rome was Greek speaking for two centuries, and so was the Church in Gaul. At first, then, the Gospels were circulated in the original language throughout the greater portion of the Empire, but an important exception was the great Roman colony of North Africa. That was purely Latin speaking. It was largely leavened with Christianity in the earliest days, and translations were wanted there almost at once. Nowadays, Mohammedanism having spread along the African coast to the Atlantic, we have a notion that Algiers and Tunis are " Eastern." But in Roman days the East ended with Egypt and a very Western West began next door in Proconsular Africa, now Algiers. That is why St. Athanasius of Alexandria is an Eastern Father and St. Augustine of Hippo a Western.

This early need for Latin translations in North Africa produced a great many, and by the end of the second century there was a popular Latin Bible in North Africa which has come to be known as the *Old Latin*. It was crude and rough, and the Roman Christians who knew the original Greek of the Gospels did not easily tolerate it, so a version revised with reference to the Greek was produced in North Italy. It is called the Italic version. But by the days of St. Jerome the copies of the Latin Bible were all badly in need of authoritative correction, the versions had got mixed, all books were hand copied and the scribes had failed to keep anything like a pure text. This was the situation in which Pope Damasus asked St. Jerome to make a new and careful revision of the Old Latin. He did so, but his corrections were so many that it was practically a new version and roused a great hostility against him. People regarded him as a dangerous innovator, and this charge combined with the disagreeable object lesson of his ascetic dress and life and his unsparing attacks on the luxury of the wealthier clergy and laity, made him easily the most unpopular man in Rome.

You remember my description of the luxury of Rome and of the group of devout ladies who were living the lives of ascetic religious in the world with the palace of Marcella as the headquarters of the movement. Jerome had stayed for the Council in the Palace on the Aventine, and when the Council was over and Jerome had become secretary to the Pope, Marcella asked him to remain and become adviser to the ascetic movement. He remained and became its controller, and the thin, swarthy-faced man in the ascetic's rough brown robe became a living and a very sharp-tongued rebuke to Rome. Rome had hated the ascetic movement among the ladies and it was not sorry to have a single figure to level its abuse at. Jerome became a target, but he cannot be said to have represented the target's passivity.

Since his earlier days in Rome the circle had received many notable additions, among them, and the most important of them all, the Lady Paula and her family. Years before, Paula had been a painted and jewelled sympathizer, now she was an associate and wearing the ascetic dress. She was of the highest rank and enormously wealthy. Her husband had lately died, she was only thirty-five, and her grief had brought her into the heart of the religious circle. Paula had five children, Blesilla, Paulina, Eustochium, Rufina, and one little boy Toxotius. Paulina was a beautiful, strong young

Christian ; Eustochium had been brought up by Marcella. She was a natural ascetic and longed to become a Church virgin, a step which so far no aristocratic young lady had taken. Rufina and Toxotius were children. There remains Blesilla, and it is upon her story that all this tale hinges.

Blesilla had made an unhappy marriage, but her husband died after seven months, and very soon his young widow was the gayest of the gay. While Marcella, Paula and Eustochium were collating Greek texts and learning Hebrew under the tutelage of Jerome, Blesilla was flitting from party to party, much petted by the worldly as the only sensible member of her family. Then Blesilla fell ill and nearly died of fever. At the crisis our Lord spoke to her and bade her arise and go forth. She recovered, and believed her recovery to be miraculous. She became a religious, assumed the habit of a Church widow, and modelled her life and household on that of Marcella. Rome was infuriated, and Jerome defended Blesilla in an open letter to Marcella. " The widow's pale face and brown robe," said Jerome, " offend the eyes of the heathen, and the eyes of Christians too who paint their cheeks with rouge and their eyelashes with antimony, those whose plastered faces look like idols, who, if in a moment of absent-mindedness they shed a tear, create a furrow in the paint all the way down the cheek, who trick out their heads with other people's hair, enamel a bygone youth upon the wrinkles of age, and affect a virgin timidity in the midst of a group of grandchildren." The Archbishop of Canterbury has said that he dislikes shingling, but he would have made himself very unpopular if he had spoken thus of the follies of our time, and the smart set did not love Jerome.

Two men came forward to fight Jerome. Helvidius was a layman and a lawyer, and there are thousands of laymen in England to-day like Helvidius in temper and outlook. He tried to undermine the ascetics by writing a book asserting that the "brethren of the Lord" were Our Lady's children, a book to which Jerome wrote a famous reply. Jovinian was an ex-monk with all an ex-monk's bitterness and much of the modern Protestant controversialist about him. He denied Our Lady's perpetual virginity, and attacked the honour paid to celibacy by the Church. He objected also to the honour paid to the Saints and their relics, and to the practice of burning altar lights in the daytime : in fact, Jovinian was the usual Protestant objector of modern times.

I often wonder whether it would not be a good thing if Catholics stood up to these gentry as Jerome stood up to Jovinian. He flayed him alive in a book of scorching epigram, which laid such stress on the glory of virginity that St. Augustine had to write a book on the good of marriage in order to redress the balance a little.

Party spirit over the matter of asceticism rose still higher a little later when the Lady Eustochium took the veil. Some of us might have thought that it would be best to lie quiet for a little and let popular indignation subside. Not so Jerome. He wrote Eustochium a public letter of congratulation in which he castigates the luxury and worse of a large section of the clergy of that time.

47

I will give you St. Jerome's description of a typical clergyman of the period.

"He is anxious about his dress, whether it is well perfumed, whether his shoes of soft leather are without a wrinkle; his hair is curled with the tongs, his fingers glitter with rings, he walks on tip-toe lest the wet road should soil the soles of his shoes. He is most diligent in visiting, he almost pushes his way into the bedchambers of people before they are awake. If he happens to see a cushion, a pretty napkin or piece of furniture, he praises it, he admires it, he handles it, he complains that he does not possess such things, he not so much begs it as extorts it, and everybody is afraid of the city gossip. Chastity he hates, fasting he hates, what he loves is the smell of dinner and his weakness is roast sucking-pig." Entirely deserved perhaps, but likely to make the writer unpopular with his brethren.

Pope Damasus was nearing his end. A strong minority determined to try to get Jerome elected Pope, a strong majority swore that that should never be. And the majority won, but by very dishonourable means. Blesilla fell ill and died, and at her great public funeral Paula broke down and was carried back to her palace in a dead faint. The sight of Blesilla's corpse and Paula's prostration roused the mob to fury. "See this mother," they cried, "who weeps for the daughter she has killed with fasting. Let us clear the accursed race of monks out of the city. Let us stone them—let us throw them into the Tiber. It is they who have led this miserable mother astray."

Given similar circumstances and a British mob would say the same things to-day.

A month after this Damasus died, and then Jerome's enemies had their revenge. They accused him of immoral relations with Paula. The story spread like wildfire—the ascetic Jerome, champion of virginity, was hooted in the streets. But the charge was soon seen to be preposterous. Jerome and Paula were completely exonerated, although of course there remained a group of people who shook their heads and whispered that there was something in it after all.

Great good came out of this evil, for now Jerome determined to forsake the world for ever, and Paula decided to follow him.

Six months after the death of Pope Damasus, Jerome set sail for the Holy Places. A party of Priests and Monks accompanied him. The new Pope and a great body of distinguished people escorted him to his ship. He spoke his farewell to Rome in a touching letter to the Lady Asella.

" I have written these lines, dear lady, on the eve of going abroad weeping and mourning, but I thank my God that I am worthy of the hatred of the world. They call me a malefactor ; I, the servant of Christ, accept the title. They call me Magician, so the Jews called my Lord ; a Seducer, so they called the Apostle.

" No temptation has taken me but such as is common to man.

" And what is it after all which I, a soldier of the Cross, have suffered ? The infamy of a false accusation has been cast on me, but I know that it is through good report and through evil report one must come to the kingdom of heaven.

" Salute Paula and Eustochium, mine in Christ

whether the world will or no. Salute Albina my mother, Marcella my sister, Marcellina, the holy Felicitas, and say to them we shall all stand before the judgment seat of Christ. There it shall be seen in what spirit we have lived. Remember me, illustrious example of purity and virginity, and let thy prayers soothe for me the stormy sea."

II

St. Jerome was nearly forty years of age when he left Rome for ever, or, to quote his more picturesque phrase, " He shook off the dust of Babylon, the scarlet whore of the Apocalypse." He had been abominably treated and he was furiously angry. He must have supposed his career of usefulness ended. As a matter of fact, God was taking him away from duties which others could perform in order that he might execute a task of which he alone was capable. He was taken from Rome that he might give the Bible to the Western Church.

He had been accused of immoral relations with Paula. It was characteristic of the courage of that age in such matters that the rejoinder which the two made to the world was to make a life partnership in the state of Holy Religion and to live side by side as Monk and Nun until their deaths. As a preliminary to this they proposed to make a pilgrimage together to the Holy Places and a visit to the great centres of the ascetic life in the desert of Egypt.

For the moment Paula, not Jerome, is the protagonist of our tale. For the next nine months during which Jerome prayed and studied in Antioch, Paula was making

her arrangements to leave Rome with a company of
young women which should form the nucleus of her
future Convent. She was to leave all her children except
Eustochium behind her, and among them she divided a
portion of her gigantic wealth. She made the most
careful arrangements for their welfare in every way.
The rest of her means she retained for the purposes of
her project. There is a pathetic picture among Jerome's
writings of the embarkation of Paula and Eustochium
at the port of Rome, of the great concourse of relations
and friends on the quay and her little children Toxotius
and Rufina watching their mother with unspeakable grief
as her ship parted from the land. The travellers landed
at Cyprus and stayed with the Bishop Epiphanius
who lived a monastic life of the cultured Benedictine sort.
Paula examined his rule and method of life, but her bent
was for something severer than this.

They reached Antioch in mid-Autumn, and hiring asses
and pack-mules they set off at once in Jerome's company
to visit the Holy Places of Palestine. They went, it is
supposed, by the coast route, rounding the headland of
Carmel and up from Cæsarea to Jerusalem. During the
days of Turkish rule this tract of country lay in ruins,
but then the greater part of it was superbly cultivated,
thickly populated, and intersected by magnificent roads
with the best posting arrangements. Judæa was already
an exception to this. It had never recovered its treatment by Titus and afterwards by Hadrian. The high
and barren tableland, so like the Peak of Derbyshire,
was already looking very much as it looks to-day.
Jerusalem itself had been twice destroyed since our Lord's
time. The city Jerome and Paula found was the smart

modern Roman city which Hadrian had built 240 years
before. Constantine had uncovered the site of the
Sepulchre sixty years before and had built the Basilicas
of the Resurrection and of Calvary. These, with the
Church of Mount Zion which covered the site of the
Upper Chamber—a site continually venerated because
the little building had survived Hadrian's destruction—
these were then as now the principal points of interest.

The Governor of Jerusalem sent a ceremonial escort
to meet the great Lady Paula, but she declined it and
entered Jerusalem riding on her donkey like the humblest
of wayfarers. The pilgrims went to a modest lodging
where Rufinus and Melania, who had been ruling
convents on the Mount of Olives for some years, greeted
them with joy. Jerome describes the tense emotion
with which they venerated the Holy Places, and in the
cave of Bethlehem Paula made her great resolution.
" Here be my rest," she cried, " for it is the country of
my Lord. Here will I dwell since my Saviour chose it,
and my seed shall serve Him."

From Jerusalem the party went south by the land
route, crossed the isthmus of Suez into Egypt and proceeded to Alexandria. So Abraham went and Joseph
and the Patriarchs and Jeroboam: so went the Holy
Family. It is a barren route, until lately full of difficulty
and hardships : it crossses the canal at Kantara.

Alexandria, like Rome and Antioch, was now at the
height of its splendour and presented an appearance of
magnificence which we cannot even imagine. It had
been from early Christian days a centre of sacred learning,
learning which had been affected in its outlook by the
broad philosophical Judaism of the dispersion of which

Alexandria was the headquarters. Jerome and Paula were deeply interested in meeting the heads of the Church in Alexandria, but they only stayed there long enough to organize the expedition which had been the principal object of their visit to Africa, the expedition to visit the monks of the Egyptian desert. You must imagine their large and well-furnished caravan crossing vast expanses of billowy sand, laced together here and there by scanty stiff grasses, towards three ranges of barren mountains.

The country became more terrible as they advanced. In the Nitrian valley at the foot of the Nitrian Mountain, the sait fog, which filled it at night, crystallized at sunrise and fell in crystals of salt, while the sharp spikes of the formations of nitre in the soil pierced the pilgrims' shoes. But from the valley of Natron there was still a day and a night's journey across the intervening range to the objective of the whole expedition, the Dry valley. In the greater part of the Dry valley not a blade of grass was to be seen, the pitiless sun blazed all day upon a scene as barren as the landscape of the moon. It must be remembered that where the desert is cultivated it is very fruitful. The Convent of St. Catherine at Mount Sinai is very similarly placed to-day, and that has palms and greenery inside its walls. I imagine there must have been some cultivated soil in the Dry valley, and of course water was procurable or life could not have existed there. But that was all: life was just possible in this awful place, and there whole choirs of ascetics lived, while in the dependent cells dwelt hundreds of solitaries.

The reception of Jerome and Paula by the great Monastery of the Dry Valley must have been a great

53

scene. The Bishop of Heliopolis had gone there with
a large party of clergy to welcome them, and now a great
procession descended towards them, the Bishop and his
Chaplains, a multitude of monks and a great company
of hermits. As they came down they chanted psalms,
and so at length they led the pilgrims back into the great
church on the top of the hill. The church was surrounded by a town of religious; a town with all the
activities necessary for the preservation of life, but with
all its other activities given to the worship and praise of
God, and intercession for the world. Mass was sung
on Saturdays and Sundays. There were eight priests
attached to the great church, but only the senior priest
ever said Mass. All the monks and solitaries came to
Mass and if a hermit did not appear some of the brethren
went at once to his cell to see what illness had seized him.
The interiors of the monasteries the travellers were not
allowed to visit.

From the City of the Saints the travellers went out to
visit the cells of the hermits who lived in the distant parts
of the mountain. The form of their asceticism varied:
one was walled up, another lived in the open always and
had no cell at all, another lived in total darkness. They
visited the celebrated Serapion. He lived in a hole at
the bottom of a narrow crack in the rocks, the mouth of
which was concealed by spiny brushwood. He was
covered with hair like a wild animal and had only a
narrow cloth round his waist. The story of Serapion was
as follows: He had been a young gentleman of good birth
at Rome, the sort of boy who belongs to the Bath Club,
who shoots in the autumn, hunts in the winter and
dances in the spring. Now there were two great variety

artistes in Rome, a man and a woman, who were living in sin together. They toured the country with a big entertainment. It was a very popular show, and very indecent. For these two people, who probably had charm and some good qualities, Serapion felt a great compassion, and he did for them what Monsignor Benson's hero in *None Other Gods* tried to do for the two vagrants, the Major and Gertie: he threw in his lot with them in order to save their souls. He sold himself to them as a slave and became one of their licentious troupe. After a time he achieved his object. He converted them both, and they were both baptized and abandoned all their evil ways. They then offered Serapion his freedom, but Serapion refused to accept it: instead he brought to them a sum of money. It was the price they had originally paid for him. " This belongs to you," he said; "now I have cost you nothing, I leave you in search of what God gives me further to do, but I leave you with a great gain, I have gained your souls."

After a time of reflection Serapion felt himself called to the solitary life and he buried himself in the Egyptian desert. Paula, the beautiful Roman lady, and Serapion, the once comely Roman boy, now a tawny wild beast in appearance, speaking together of Roman acquaintances in the crack of a rock in the Mountain of the Saints! It is a great picture. Paula's resolution to found a Convent in Bethlehem was shaken. Seriously she debated whether she and her young women should not become solitaries of the Egyptian desert. Jerome tells us that in the end the love of the Holy Places proved the stronger motive, and taking a tender farewell of the

wonderful dwellers in the wilderness the travellers left
Egypt and returned to Bethlehem.

Nowadays as one rides up from the Dead Sea to Bethlehem crowning the high stony ridge, the enormous fortress-
like buildings of Jerome and Paula's Convents, with the
Church of the Nativity mixed up in them, remind one a
little of the Convent and Church of San Francesco at
Assisi. When Jerome and Paula arrived at Bethlehem
in 386 to spend the rest of their lives there, only the
Church itself stood over the limestone cave which had
been an outside storehouse and stable of the big Khan
at the time of our Lord's birth. It is interesting to know
that the nave of the church is unchanged, it is all just
as it was in 386. The choir over the cave itself has been
partly rebuilt and altered.

The travellers got big lodgings for their party and
proceeded to develop their plans. They bought the
ground round the church with room enough on it for
Jerome's Convent for men, Paula's two Convents of
women, and a guest house for travellers, so that, as
Paula said, " If Joseph and Mary come again to Bethlehem they may find an inn to lodge in." It took three
years to put the buildings up. Jerome is a model to
us in the matter of the use of time. We should have
been tempted to say that we had enough to do in super-
intending the building of the Convents. Not so Jerome.
He began his religious and studious life at once. He got
possession of a cave near the cave of the Nativity, put his
books and papers there, engaged scribes and set to work.
Up to this time he had never been more than three years
in one place since his boyhood, but from this place he
never stirred again. He had worn the brown frock of a

hermit for years. He always fasted till sunset, only ate bread and vegetables, kept the Canonical hours regularly, and spent the rest of his time in prayer and study. He at once opened a school for the children of Bethlehem and had them taught gratis. For himself, he set himself to perfect his Hebrew and Chaldee, for he had conceived the gigantic plan of translating the Old Testament from the original Hebrew into Latin. At this time the Septuagint, the Greek version of the Old Testament, was being used by the Church, but it is often rather a paraphrase than a translation. It was arranged that Jerome's Latin should be turned into Greek for the use of Orientals. He got the help of learned Rabbis and set to work, throwing off a number of minor works during the two years he was preparing the greater. He was an astounding worker, and Paula and Eustochium worked almost as hard as Jerome. Both had made themselves elegant Greek and Hebrew scholars and the two ladies came and worked hard in Jerome's cave every day. It was no play-work, it was literary work of the hardest, most unremitting kind at which the three persevered. Truly they were a marvellous trio.

As soon as the monasteries were ready they were full; people crowded to them to try their vocations. Paula proved a heaven-born Mother Superior of her three bands of nuns, who were divided as to their refectory and their work, but united in the choir. Apparently they only heard Mass once a week—on Sundays—they said the whole office, the night office was said regularly. Jerome's monks were mostly students like himself, but they had a hospital under their care and this hospital was the thorn in the flesh to Jerome. The continual stream of pilgrims kept it full, and it was a very distracting and harassing bit of work.

It will be convenient to speak here of the general scope of Jerome's work during the rest of his life. He wrote a number of minor treatises, a number of orations, a vast number of long and valuable epistles, but his fame is connected with his controversies and his translation of the Bible. I can only just touch on the controversies, but you must remember that they occupy a very big place indeed in his life.

No great writer has so divided Catholic opinion as Origen, the greatest of the Alexandrians; he was very original, very learned, very speculative. Was he orthodox? It has become clear that in several respects his speculations ran counter to the judgment of the Church, but the Church would seem to have thought more tenderly of Origen than of any man who has overstepped the bounds of her teaching. Origen had died in 253. The controversy about him had died down for a while after his death, but now it broke out again with great violence. Broadly speaking, the Western part of the Church tended to censure Origen, and the Eastern part of the Church to praise him. Jerome and Paula at Bethlehem and their friends, Rufinus and Melania on the Mount of Olives, were Westerns living in the East, but they had all felt a great admiration for Origen. His work as a Biblical scholar had endeared him to Jerome, and Jerome had used Origen a good deal, but always with careful discrimination. The Bishop of Jerusalem, Bishop John, who was an able though not deeply learned man, was a warm friend of Rufinus. Jerome agreed with them in their appreciation of the great Origen. By this time the controversy was raging in the monasteries of Egypt, and an organized attack on Origenism was begun. A theologian called Aterbius, who had become a professional agitator against the opinions of Origen, came to Jerusalem and accused the Bishop, Jerome and Rufinus of heresy. Jerome cleared himself passionately, and the terms of his repudiation made the Bishop and Rufinus very angry. A little later Epiphanius, the learned and saintly Bishop of Salamis, came to Jerusalem and stayed as he always did in the Bishop's Palace. The Bishop asked him to speak in the Church of the Holy Sepulchre next morning. Epiphanius did so, and the sermon was an attack upon Origen, which the Bishop felt to be an attack upon himself. Bishop John writhed on his throne for some minutes and then sent the Archdeacon into the pulpit to ask Epiphanius to stop. The large congregation, however, crowded round Epiphanius at the end of the Liturgy and kissed his feet and implored his blessing. Epiphanius was a miracle worker and he had a reputation like that of Father John of Kronstadt. Well, here was an awkward situation. Luncheon at the Palace that day must have been uncomfortable. That afternoon Bishop John was to preach and he made an indirect reply: he attacked the errors of the extreme opponents of Origen. When he finished Epiphanius got up in his stall and said, " I agree with all that: it is right we should condemn both the errors of Origen and of the unbalanced extremists who oppose him." People laughed all round, and the Bishop of Jerusalem felt he had come off second best. Two days afterwards Bishop John made a detailed profession of his faith in the course of a sermon, and turning to Epiphanius asked him whether that were not the

Catholic Religion. Epiphanius said he had not noted any error, but on reflection afterwards he felt there had been several, and that he had been made to compromise himself in public. He went straight off to Bethlehem without saying good-bye to anyone in Jerusalem and told Jerome he meant to break off communion with the Bishop of Jerusalem. Jerome and Paula did all they could to compose matters, but Epiphanius was determined, and soon after he wrote to all the monasteries of Palestine calling upon them to go out of communion with John. This letter was the sword which divided Jerome and Paula from Rufinus and Melania. Jerome and Paula sided with Epiphanius, Rufinus and Melania with John.

The Bishop of Jerusalem now cut off Jerome and Paula and their communities from communion and would not even let them hear Mass. Jerome was a priest, but he had never said Mass, and he refused to say it under these circumstances. It was a terrible situation, solved in an irregular way, not uncommon in that age. Paulinian, Jerome's brother, was sent with letters to Epiphanius at this juncture. Epiphanius took him and forcibly ordained him and sent him back to say Mass in the communities at Bethlehem. The Bishop of Jerusalem now formally excommunicated anybody who received Paulinian as a priest. As the majority of the people of Bethlehem sided with the monasteries, this involved them. John then tried to get Jerome banished by the State, but he did not succeed and Jerome was left in his monastery from which he conducted a controversial campaign against his former friend Rufinus, which entirely puts the eloquence of Mr. Lloyd

George in his most combative moments into the shade.

The state authorities after a while interfered in a pacific direction. The Governor of Palestine came to Bethlehem to mediate, but the Bishop of Jerusalem would not come. He would not appeal to his own Metropolitan, the Bishop of Cæsarea, because the Bishop of Jerusalem was not at all satisfied with his position as a suffragan of Cæsarea. He appealed to Alexandria and Rome, and the Bishop of Alexandria, who was having a very hard time of it between the two parties in his own Patriarchate and at the time was siding with the Origenists, undertook to judge the dispute. Jerome was rightly indignant at the affair being dealt with by a neighbouring Metropolitan who was himself a party in the case. " Behold the loyalty of this Bishop," he says, "who invokes as judge of a dispute the man who is the author of it. See his obedience to the laws of the Church who on a question involving discipline as well as dogma invokes a foreign tribunal."

The Patriarch of Alexandria sent a legate to represent him, and he sent two letters, one to Jerome and one to the Bishop of Jerusalem in advance of the legate. But he made a comical mistake; he put the letters into the wrong envelopes, and when Jerome had read the letter intended for Jerusalem he saw that the case had already been prejudged. I do not envy the legate, Isidore, when he arrived at the Convent at Bethlehem. However, negotiations were opened, and while they were still in progress the Patriarch of Alexandria, who had been halting between two opinions, came down unexpectedly but quite definitely on Jerome's side of the fence. He wrote further letters to Jerome and Epiphanius thanking

them for their work as defenders of the Faith. Poor
Bishop John climbed down, and Jerome met him half-way.
The interdict was lifted. John recognized Paulinian,
Jerome and Rufinus embraced each other at the Holy
Sepulchre, and both communicated in Bishop John's
Eucharist. Bishop John became Warden of Jerome's
monasteries and all was sunshine once more.

But the controversy was shaking other Churches, and
alas! it threw St. Jerome and St. John Chrysostom
into opposite parties, and it is a moving thought and one
which it is useful to ponder over that St. Jerome was of
the party which sent St. Chrysostom to exile and to death.

I wish I could say that here the Origenistic controversy
ended so far as Jerome was concerned. But it did not.
Rufinus left Jerusalem soon after his reconciliation and
returned to Rome where he became a theological lecturer.
After a time he published what professed to be a translation of a work of Origen's, but in which, as a matter
of fact, Rufinus had omitted or modified the more
objectionable passages and added some orthodox sen-
tences here and there. In the preface to this he paid a
high compliment to Jerome. He developed a system of
teaching in which he used expurgated Origen and com-
mended it to Rome by quoting Jerome's commendations
of portions of Origen in earlier days. This put Jerome
in the wrong with Rome. " If Origen did not say worse
things than this," said Roman Society, " why should he
be condemned ? and see too how much Jerome has to
say in his favour." Jerome could not be expected to
stand this. He made a proper translation of the treatise
of Origen and sent it to Rome with a repudiation of the
position Rufinus had attributed to him.

Rome was in flames, the Pope Siricius refused to censure Rufinus, but his successor Anastasius did censure him indirectly. Rufinus went to his home at Aquileia and wrote an Apologia which was an attack on Jerome. Jerome replied with an Apologia which was an attack on Rufinus. During this life the breach between the old friends was never healed.

III

It will be best to finish what I can say about the controversies in which St. Jerome was engaged, and then to say a word about his work on the Bible, before we return to the story of his daily life up to the time of his death.

You remember how Helvidius, a lawyer, and Jovinian, an ex-monk, had attacked Jerome's asceticism in Rome long before, and aspects of the Catholic teaching about Our Lady and the honour paid to celibacy. Years afterwards Jerome found himself in conflict with similar tendencies in the person of a Spanish priest, Vigilantius. Vigilantius wrote a treatise against the practices connected with the Communion of Saints very much on the lines of the earlier treatise of Jovinian. These three men represent a revulsion against the Catholic theory of Sanctity, of which at this time the flesh-subduing and world-renouncing elements were excessively prominent.

Vigilantius' heresy was repugnant to all the tendencies of Jerome's nature, and his reply to him is extremely fierce and bitter. He is least attractive when he is defending the ideals he had so steadfastly pursued. St. Jerome's controversy with St. Augustine is more interesting, and

like the controversy with Bishop John has strong touches
of comedy in it. St. Augustine was a good deal younger
than St. Jerome, he had become a Christian late in life
and was the brilliant new star in the Church's firmament
when Jerome was a man of long settled reputation.
The point of the controversy was a small one. It was
the interpretation of the dispute between St. Peter and
St. Paul at Antioch. This the Eastern commentators
had regarded as a dramatic scene arranged between the
two Apostles to demonstrate to the converts that they
should no longer keep the Jewish law, and Jerome had
accepted this view in his commentary on the Epistle to
the Galatians. The view was new to St. Augustine,
and when he found it in Jerome's book it shocked him
very much. He wrote a strong letter to St. Jerome,
the sort of letter it is not pleasant to receive. For nine
years there was no acknowledgment of the letter for the
odd reason that Jerome had not received it. The priest
to whom it was entrusted never completed his journey; he
was recalled to a Bishopric and soon afterwards died.
He never told Augustine that he had failed to deliver
the letter, but he showed the letter to several people who
copied it. As years went on this strong piece of criticism
of a bit of St. Jerome's exegesis was being circulated
throughout the West while Jerome did not know of its
existence. At last St. Augustine discovered the truth
and he wrote Jerome another long letter. You and I
would have been very apologetic and conciliatory, not so
St. Augustine: the second letter was as vigorous as the
first. And this is hardly believable, but it is quite true;
this second letter also was never delivered. The messenger, when questioned why he had not fulfilled his

task, said that at the last moment his heart failed him, he was afraid of the sea. And he too disseminated the second letter, again without Augustine's knowledge. A deacon called Sysinnius read the letter in an island in the Adriatic, and some time afterwards during a visit to Bethlehem he told Jerome that Augustine was attacking him. Happily Jerome had his temper in hand; he waited patiently to see if there was any explanation. Augustine now heard what had happened and he wrote his explanation—letters which were meant to be for private discussion had unfortunately been made public. Augustine hoped Jerome would deal as freely with his own writings. Jerome rejoined somewhat tartly that he knew but little of the writings of Augustine. If he should ever know more, he felt sure he should be able to oblige Augustine with a good deal of criticism of them. St. Augustine replied with great respect and courtesy. He warmly praised St. Jerome's New Testament translations but begged him not to publish a new version of the Old Testament from the Hebrew. He felt sure it would upset the faithful terribly. Indeed, he described how a North African congregation had been scandalized by Jerome's new version of Jonah which the Rector had read. Jerome had substituted " ivy " for " gourd," and when the Rector read " ivy " the congregation shouted " gourd," and continued to shout it until the Rector reverted to the translation they were accustomed to. The Rector would have had no congregation left, Augustine said, if he had continued to say " ivy." It is an interesting fact that the greatest of the Latin Fathers tried to stop the issue of the Vulgate on conservative grounds. But Jerome and Augustine were determined

E

to be friends. Jerome came apparently to accept Augustine's view about the Apostolic dispute at Antioch, and happily Augustine did not lead an attack on the new Latin Bible.

Towards the end of Jerome's life the two Fathers found common ground in opposition to Pelagianism. Pelagius was a Welshman named Morgan, a monk who held and taught a very defective conception of the relation of the human will to sin. But we must not discuss Pelagianism here: it belongs to the life of St. Augustine who was its chief opponent.

At intervals amid all these controversies, the greatest work of Jerome's life was proceeding, though somewhat fitfully, his translation of the Old Testament from Hebrew into Latin. This translation of his now forms the bulk of the Vulgate or common Bible of the Western Church.

The rest of the present Vulgate is derived as follows: Wisdom, Ecclus., 1 & 2 Macc., and Baruch are the old version which existed before St. Jerome's day. The Psalter is the old version revised by St. Jerome by reference to the Greek Old Testament. The books of Judith and Tobit are a hasty and free translation by Jerome ; they were each the work of a single day. Of the New Testament, the Gospels are from the old Latin version revised with reference to the Greek original by St. Jerome, and the rest of the New Testament is also St. Jerome's revision of the old Latin, but it was done much less completely than the Gospels.

St. Jerome's translation of the Old Testament from the original Hebrew was not undertaken by order of any ecclesiastical authority. He did it from a sense of the need of the work and with the warm encouragement of some of his friends. It was by no means the Vulgate or common version for some time; at first only some of the learned appreciated it and the majority disliked it extremely because it proposed to take away from them the text they had come to love.

Indeed this, the greatest task of St. Jerome's life, was an extremely ungrateful one, and he was intensely sensitive to the attacks which were levelled against it. At times his friends had to extort fresh portions of it from him. Somewhere he speaks of wanting to get it off his hands that he might return to his commentaries, and in the preface to the translation of Esther which completed his colossal task, he makes no reference to its conclusion. But Jerome was giving the Bible to mankind —his work meant no less than this, and it is fitting that the task should have been accomplished with pain, amid misunderstanding and hostility.

It remains for me to say something further of life in the Convents of Bethlehem and to tell the tale of the later years of Jerome and of Paula. The life was splendidly real and thorough. The nuns praised God and prayed, worked and made clothes for the poor. They all had to know the Psalter by heart and to learn a fresh bit of Scripture every day. Paula was a very strict, but also a very wise and tender superior. She knew how to be lenient at the right moment, and she was far stricter with herself than with anyone else. She kept up a constant correspondence with Rome. Paulina, her young daughter, was married to Pammachius during the first year of her mother's religious life. Paula's boy, Toxotius, grew up a bitter young Pagan. He was engaged to Laeta, the daughter of the Pagan Pontiff, Albinus. But Laeta was

a Christian, and before long she converted Toxotius
who became devout and good. Three years after they
began their life at Bethlehem, Paula, Eustochium and
Jerome made a great effort to get Marcella to come and
join them. They give a delightful picture of their life.

"There is no arrogance here," they say, "and no
disdain, the only strife is which can be most humble.
The newest comer is the first in estimation. There is
no distinction of habit and no care about it. Fasts do
not exalt anyone, neither abstinence is blamed, nor is
moderate abundance condemned, we are almost entirely
free from quarrelling. Come to the little city of Christ
and the lodging of Mary. All is rustic. The silence is
only broken by psalms ; wherever you turn, the plough-
man, holding the plough, sings alleluias, the toiling
reaper cheers his labour with psalms, the vinedresser,
pruning the vine with his curved knife, sings something of
David. These are the ballads of this country, these its
love songs, this the shepherd's pipe, these its rustic
sports." "Here," adds Jerome, "bread and herbs
grown with our own hands, and milk, rural delicacies,
afford us humble but healthy food. Living thus, sleep
does not overtake us in prayer, satiety does not interfere
with study. In summer the trees afford us shade. In
autumn the air is cool and the fallen leaves give us a
quiet resting-place. In spring the field is clothed with
flowers, and we sing our psalms the sweeter among the
singing of the birds. When the winter cold and snow
come we have no lack of wood, and I watch or sleep
warm enough."

So charming a picture drew many of the Roman
aristocracy to Bethlehem. I suppose travelling has

never since been so luxurious and easy as it was in the days
of the Roman Empire. It was one perfectly organized
world with a common language and a wonderful system
of couriers, inns and posting. In the rapid travelling
of to-day one shifts for oneself and leaves one's native
tongue behind at Dover. There is probably more
nervous effort in travelling to-day from London to
Naples than there was in travelling from Rome to Bethlehem in the days of St. Jerome.

Among the Roman ladies who visited Bethlehem there
arrived in 395 the Lady Fabiola. She had married a
bad man, divorced him, married another, and was now
living separated from him. Her miseries had brought
her to God, and her penitence and piety were greatly
strengthened by her retreat with Paula and her nuns.

While Fabiola was at Bethlehem the terror of the Huns
drew near. They were not to descend on central Europe
for some time yet. Rome was to experience Alaric and
the Goths before she was attacked by Attila and his Huns.
But now, in 395, the Huns had crossed the Caucasus
and were besieging Antioch and threatening Jerusalem.
Jerome brought his communities down to the seashore
and encamped them there, and he chartered ships to lie
off the land in waiting, that he might send away his people
into safety if the danger became pressing. But the Huns
did not advance, they halted before the Lebanon and
turned home again ; so Jerome and Paula brought their
communities back to Bethlehem.

Fabiola, however, went back to Rome, leaving her
case of conscience—a woman who had divorced and
married again—with Jerome. Jerome sent a letter
after her to Rome, bidding her do penance for her sin.

The penance of Fabiola produced a great stir in Rome.
She had only done what the State allowed, and she was a
noble of the nobles. But Fabiola stood in penance on
the steps of the Lateran, in mourning robe and dishevelled
hair, her head sprinkled with ashes. Rome looked on and
wondered. Then Fabiola sold all her goods, built
hospitals, and became a nursing sister of the suffering
poor. Two years later, Paula's third daughter, Paulina,
died in giving birth to her first child, and her young husband Pammachius was inconsolable. She had left him
her wealth with orders to distribute it among the poor.
Pammachius decided to give away most of his own at
the same time. All day long on the day of Paulina's
funeral Pammachius fed the poor at long tables stretched
the length of the basilica of St. Peter's at Rome. As
each guest left he was given new clothes and a considerable sum of money. Pammachius became a monk,
and he took his seat in the Senate amid the laughter of the
Pagans, wearing habit and cord.

It was about this time that a daughter was born to
Toxotius and Laeta, Paula's son and daughter-in-law.
Laeta, remember, was a fervent Christian, although the
daughter of Albinus, the pontiff of the old Pagan state
religion. Albinus was really a polite free-thinker, and
he had allowed his children to be Pagan or Christian,
as they pleased. This was the end of the old Pagan
religion of Rome, for Alaric the Goth swept it all away
a few years later at the conquest of the city.

The last picture we have of a Pagan pontiff is in an
epistle of Jerome's, and it is a very pretty and friendly
one. He pictures Albinus surrounded by his Christian
children and grandchildren, nursing the baby Paula

on his knee, and listening with delight at her attempt to say the first word her mother taught her, "Alleluia." The baby whom Albinus nursed closed the eyes of Jerome.

Soon after this Paula began to fail. Worn out by her labours and austerities she failed year by year, and towards the end of the year 403 she took to her bed for the last time. Jerome describes the intense grief of Eustochium, the tenderness of her nursing, and her agonized prayers in the Church of the Nativity that her mother's life might be spared. Paula died in February, 404. She died in public and in state as befits a great ecclesiastic. The convent was filled with choirs of monks and nuns ; all the bishops of the neighbourhood were assembled in the death chamber; the corridors were thronged with priests. She died, says Jerome, as though she were going to visit friends. " Lord, I have loved the habitation of Thy house," and " O how amiable are thy dwellings," were the psalms she murmured at the end. At the very last Jerome asked her tenderly if she was in pain, and she answered him in Greek. " I am in no trouble. I see all things before me in tenderness and peace." At the very end she made the sign of the cross on her lips, and passed so nobly that there was no grief, only the chanting of the psalms in many different tongues. Bishops carried Paula's bier into the centre of the Church of the Nativity, where she lay as though asleep, while the psalter was chanted around her in Hebrew, Greek, Latin and Syriac.

Jerome was heartbroken for a while and could not take up his usual tasks, but at last Eustochium came to him and said, " My father, this is the next book of the Bible which you and I must translate," and put into his hands the book of Ruth ; and Jerome accepted the comfort so exquisitely conveyed, and persevered once more.

During all this period appalling storm-clouds were threatening the Empire from the north. Alaric and the Goths were getting further down into Italy year by year. Four years later Alaric was at the walls of Rome. Bought off with a ransom then, he returned next year, and in 410 he sacked the city. That extraordinary luxury set in that incomparable frame was shattered into ruin. The great palaces, of which some had become sanctuaries of Christian piety, were destroyed. The nobles fled to the coast and sailed for any land to which a ship would take them. Only the Christian basilicas were respected by the Arian Goths ; into them Pagans and Christians crowded for sanctuary.

In this hideous ruin and slaughter Marcella died. She had been thrown to the ground and cruelly scourged, but was rescued by a kindly Goth, and dragged, together with her adopted child, Principia, to the shelter of St. Paul's without the walls. There, amid the shivering crowd of fugitives, lit up by the glare of the burning city, Marcella gave up her soul. Compared with the sufferings of the nobles in the sack of Rome, the guillotine of the Place de la République was an instrument of mercy. The sailors robbed them on board ship; the inhabitants of the countries in which they landed stripped them of their clothes ; the provincial authorities threw them into prison, hoping to extort ransoms; the girls of noble birth were sold as slaves into Mesopotamia and Persia. Numbers of the Christian nobles got to Bethlehem. Jerome and Eustochium gave them all they had. Never has there been such a period of horror as that of Alaric and Attila. And, curiously enough, the sack of Rome precipitated the attempt of Pelagius to weaken the doctrine of grace, just as the troubles of these times have been utilized for an attempt to weaken the doctrine of the Church. Pelagius fled to Africa and Palestine, and this brought him into contact with Augustine and Jerome, and they had to find time, notwithstanding the public distress, to defend the doctrine of grace.

The story, as I have said, belongs to the life of St. Augustine. Jerome's opposition to Pelagianism was less effective and adequate, but it nearly cost him his life. The heresy had a large following among monks, and a crowd of Pelagian monks attacked the Bethlehem monastery, slaughtered some of Jerome's community, and partly pulled down and partly burned the buildings. Jerome escaped by taking refuge in the most strongly fortified tower, but the nuns had a terrible time that night. They fled into the open country and made a wide circuit back to get to the safety of Jerome's tower. Jerome and his monks made a sally at the right moment and held up the enemy till the nuns got inside the building. But the shock of this wild night hastened the death of Eustochium. She died on the 20th September, 418 ; and the younger Paula, Toxotius' child, who had played on the knee of Albinus, the old pagan pontiff, became Abbess of Bethlehem.

Two years later St. Jerome passed to his rest. They were two years of sickness and sorrow. The old man was nearly blind, his voice had been reduced to a whisper, his body was almost transparent. He used to lift himself by a cord hung from the ceiling and whisper his office as the hours came round. Paula, friend of a third generation, nursed him tenderly till the end. Legend tells us that at the very last the great Augustine came from Hippo to Bethlehem, and that it was the hand of Augustine which administered Viaticum to Jerome. On the 30th September, 420, the soul of Jerome passed to God.

When you visit Bethlehem you will go from the cave of the Nativity through a passage cut in the living rock to the cell which Jerome called his paradise, and from which the sacred Scriptures went forth to the Western world. In a cell hard by are two tombs before which you will kneel with reverence and awe. One is the tomb of Paula and Eustochium, the other is the tomb of Jerome.

ST. AMBROSE

I

In the life of St. Ambrose we are still in the days of St. Jerome, the first years of the triumph of the Church, the first years of the downfall of the Empire. We are to look at the same period we considered in the previous papers, but from a very different point of view. St. Jerome was the son of a Norfolk squire, St. Ambrose was the son of the Viceroy of India; perhaps that expresses in our modern English terms the difference between the up-bringing of the two men. The date of the birth of neither Father is quite certain, but St. Ambrose was probably six years older than St. Jerome. The date of his birth is generally given as 340. Both Fathers diligently set themselves to minister to the needs of their time. Jerome's asceticism was a perpetual sermon as to the possibility of regaining for the spirit a complete control of the impulses of the flesh. He served society by standing apart from it. St. Ambrose was a statesman. He came of a diplomatic stock and was nurtured on diplomatic traditions. Certain families have a mission apparently to bring high Christian sentiment and conduct to the assistance of the affairs of State. We expect always to have one at least of their name in the public eye, and the name is equivalent to a type of character we could ill spare from public life. It is not, I hope, impertinent to mention in illustration such names as Gladstone, Cavendish, Lyttelton and Cecil. Ambrose was a man of such traditions. His father was Prefect of the Province of Gaul, one of the four divisions of the Empire, which was much larger than Gaul, properly so-called. The elder Ambrose was Viceroy of France, Holland, Belgium, Switzerland, Spain, Portugal and Great Britain. The Prefect of course had many palaces in different parts of the province, and we are uncertain whether Ambrose was born at Treves or Arles or Lyons, just as future ages might not be sure whether the son of a Viceroy of India had been born at Calcutta or Simla or Delhi.

This was the Prefect's third child and second son, and he determined that he should bear his own name, Ambrosius.

The Prefect was a Christian of noble life. His reputation as an administrator was very high. He belonged to an old and illustrious family which had been faithfully Christian in the time of persecution and which counted a virgin martyr of the days of Diocletian to be its greatest glory.

Sidonius Apollinaris, also a man of the governing class, writing in Gaul more than a century later, describes the household of such a man as the elder Ambrose.

" The household," he says, " like its master, keeps its charity unimpaired. The slaves are attentive, the rustics respectful, civil and content with their patron. The table feeds not only guests but dependants; there is great courtesy and greater sobriety. His horses, dogs, and hawks are the best of the countryside. He loves hunting, but will not eat the venison. He is a widower

and devotes great care to the education of his only child,
a daughter. Often he reads the Bible or has it read at
meal-times, feeding soul and body at once. The Psalms
he constantly reads or chants. In a word he is a perfect
monk in the uniform of a soldier. He is a priestly man,
and I admire him more than if he had been a priest."

How near that seems to bring the fourth and fifth centuries to us ! It might be a fragment of Addison, a sketch
of a devout, Catholic Sir Roger de Coverley. No doubt it
describes to us the atmosphere in which Ambrose was
born, although the circumstances of his early upbringing
were far more stately.

It amazes us that the baby was not baptized.

In the fourth century infant baptism was by no means
the invariable rule. But it must not be thought
that baptism was deferred from the notion that infants
were incapable of receiving the grace of the sacrament.
The reason was an acute sense of the awfulness
of baptism and the heinousness of postbaptismal sin.
You must remember that there was no Christian atmosphere in society. There was even less than there is
to-day: all the organized temptations of Paganism lay
before every young Christian in an unblushing way.
Further there had been the danger, now almost gone, of
a recrudescence of persecution and therefore of the risk
of apostasy; and, lastly, there were many places where
Catholic baptism could not be obtained from the clergy
owing to the spread of Arianism. The fear that heretical
baptism might be administered deterred many scrupulous
people of Catholic beliefs from applying for it.

So baby Ambrose was not baptized. The boy is said
to have had an air of great distinction and authority

about him which distinguished him from other children. Certainly there is something in the poise of the head and the delicacy of the features and skin in some children which make them look as though they were of better flesh and blood than the majority. Such was Ambrose from his cradle; and in harmony with this is the story of the swarm of bees. One day in the hot spring weather the baby's cradle had been put for coolness under the great stone arcades of a quadrangle of the viceregal mansion when a cloud of bees flew into the court and swarmed upon the baby's head, crawling in and out of his mouth as though it was the entrance to a hive. Mercifully the Prefect and his wife were sitting near. They stopped the nurse who would have made some futile effort to drive away the bees, and would thereby have killed the child, and waited in an agony lest the child should cry or strike out; but in a few seconds the swarm rose pyramid-like and ascended into the air until it was out of sight. The Prefect heaved a sigh of relief, and said, " If the boy lives he will be great."

Twelve happy years followed for Ambrose in the orderly household of his father. His sister Marcellina and his brother Satyrus were both older than he. Marcellina was an intensely spiritual and devout child, and her brothers regarded her with awe ; they were a pair of inseparables, two brothers who were also heart to heart chosen friends of each other.

When Ambrose was thirteen the great Prefect died, and his widow and her children found themselves in the dethroned position in which the death of a great State official leaves his family. They left the Province of Gaul and went back to Rome, where the widow took a

house in order that the boys might be matriculated at
the Roman University. The mother and brothers were
being called upon to undergo a second deprivation, and
one which is the peculiar trial of Catholic families.
Marcellina had a vocation for the religious life. At the
feet of Pope Liberius she consecrated herself to God
by a vow of virginity, and the rest of her life she spent
apart from her family in religious solitude and asceticism.

The Rome into which the Prefect's widow and her
two boys had settled was the Rome we have seen in
the story of St. Jerome. St. Jerome was beginning his
lessons at home at Stridon just then, and in the first
year of Ambrose's young life in Rome a greater than
either Jerome or he was born away in North Africa, a
baby boy to whom the names Aurelius Augustinus were
given, Augustine, son of the Pagan Patricius and the
Christian Monica.

There is one little story of Ambrose, in the first days
at Rome. The clergy came in great numbers to pay
their respects to the widow of the great Christian Prefect,
and the lady and her daughter always kissed their hands
reverentially. One day thirteen-year-old Ambrose
stretched out his hands to his mother and sister. " You
ought to kiss my hands," he said, and with such an odd
insistence and gravity that they never forgot the incident,
and ultimately told it to the Church as an unconscious
prophecy.

You remember the Rome in which the boy grew
up. It was at the supreme moment of its extent
and magnificence, as yet untouched by spoiler or
decay. It was no longer the seat of Empire, and
this had left it in the hands of the great patrician

79

houses, which were Pagan for the same reason that our
noble families in England are mostly untouched by the
Catholic revival, through a conservative disdain for
change and enthusiasm.

The Church was very strong and very rich. The
Bishop of Rome was a very important person from a civic
point of view. There were many splendid churches,
but the Pagan temples were still untouched. The Pagan
priesthood was endowed by the State ; all the old Pagan
ceremonies were still observed. The Emperor and the
imperial officials were Christian, except during Julian's
short reign, which began and ended while Ambrose was
at College, but the Senate and the nobles were defiantly
Pagan, although many ladies of their families were
Christian. You remember, too, how we filled in the
scene of the ancient Rome, of which there are still remains,
with the domestic houses which have perished, tall,
steeply gabled, built of brick, with overhanging balconies,
lining narrow, deeply-shaded streets. We imagined
the enormous, ever-moving crowds of picturesque and
dirty people, with here and there a brilliant gentleman,
while every now and then litters went through with ladies
reclining in them dressed and painted as though for the
stage.

Of the life of Ambrose in Rome we know next to
nothing. His brother and he studied hard. A staunch
Christian, although unbaptized, Ambrose grew accomplished in the whole judicial, literary and artistic tradition
of Greece and Rome. He grew to be a very accomplished and distinguished young gentleman indeed.
His social advantages brought him into contact with the
most prominent men of the day, and they thought him

worth cultivating. He showed diplomatic and administrative qualities of a marked kind.

The world of that time was comically like the English world of to-day in many respects. Pagan and Christian together transacted the affairs of the Empire and formed two mutually tolerant groups constantly brought into contact over various matters. They differ, though, from our world of to-day in one odd particular. To-day the Pagans are nearly all baptized and then the Christians were many of them not baptized. Two men represented the two groups. Symmachus, the Prefect of Rome, was a Pagan, and a magnificent governor of the city. Probus, Viceroy of the Italian Province of the Empire, was a Christian and a man of the highest character. He was immensely wealthy, and he had lavished his money on good works. Ambrose and his brother were constantly in the houses of these two great personages. Symmachus treated Satyrus like a son, and when his own son went as Quæstor to Lycaonia he sent Satyrus with him as his first secretary. Probus was devoted to Ambrose, and when the young man had finished his education Probus took him into the Prætorian prefecture, which was a sort of military Home Office, a Home Office presided over by a Lord Kitchener and run on military lines. He soon rose to the important post of legal adviser to the prefecture, and he stayed there till he was thirty-four.

Public affairs had been very uneasy during the greater part of Ambrose's life in Rome. Constantius the Arian remained Emperor during the first eight years. He was succeeded by Julian, the philosophical pervert to heathenism, but his reign and the reign of his Christian successor Jovian were short, and in 364 Valentinian became Emperor of the West, while Valens his brother ruled in the East. Valentinian was a Catholic Christian and a great emperor, who ruled with a strong hand, and knew a strong man when he saw him. He laid his hand on Ambrose and sent him from the prætorian prefecture to govern North Italy, with his palace and tribunal in Milan, then the working centre of the Western Empire.

At his parting interview with Ambrose, Probus gave him a memorable bit of advice. " Go, my son," he said, " and act not as a judge, but as a bishop."

North Italy was sad and sore from a long series of revolts, and the wise Probus suggests that they needed a light and soothing touch. But he also spoke in unconscious prophecy.

Ambrose made an immediate success at Milan. The people were ready to appreciate a strong and gentle governor. Valentinian the Emperor had ruled that neighbourhood with stern and sometimes hasty severity. He had a favourite maxim of which the people of Milan had grown tired : " Severity is the soul of justice," he used to say, " and justice is the soul of power."

Ambrose came with another maxim : " Justice is a virtue that ought to bring peace to the governed and be a shield to the oppressed." He gave himself unreservedly and tried to correct all wrongs one by one. He was so merciful in carrying out the imperial orders that even while he carried them out in their sternness he was beloved. He was boundlessly charitable and he was stainlessly pure. And still unbaptized, remember. Still untouched by baptismal grace. Ambrose at this time is a model of what a good man can be who believes in

Christ and follows Him without any recourse to the Sacraments, but Ambrose died a Catholic saint, and that he could never have been without the Sacraments.

And now we come to the great crisis in Ambrose's earlier life. He was universally adored in a city torn by faction, and by the worst of all—religious faction. Twenty years before this time Milan had been the scene of stormy debates between the Arians and the Catholics. The Arians, who acknowledged two Gods, a greater divinity and a lesser, and so destroyed the value of the Incarnation, and brought polytheism back into being ; and the Catholics, who held one God, but three subsistences in the one Being of God, the Father, the Son and the Holy Ghost. The difference was of course absolutely vital. About the *Homoousion* there could be no compromise ; no alternative formula could be tolerated. The Council of Nicæa had anathematized Arianism many years before the great dispute at Milan, but this had not prevented the poison spreading through the Empire, and in 365 some corrupt bishops had persuaded the Emperor Constans that his authority extended over matters of doctrine. Constans had therefore presided over the Catholic and Arian debate at Milan, and had given his vote to the Arians, because, as a shrewd historian has remarked, " He had the sagacity to perceive that in the nature of things that party only would be ready to ally itself with material force."

Dionysius, the Catholic Bishop of Milan, had resisted this pretension of the Emperor; he had been banished and had died in exile, and an Arian named Auxentius had been intruded into the See. Few submitted to him, and there were many discussions and even open hos-

tilities, all of which Valentinian repressed with a strong
hand when they arose.

And now, a year after Ambrose had begun his work
in Milan, Auxentius the Arian died, and the city was
plunged into a turmoil over the election of a new Bishop.
There was an Arian party, but the Catholics were determined there should not be another Arian Bishop. The
action of Valentinian, too, was a matter for anxiety. He
was in the habit of putting down excitement with a strong
hand. What would he do? It was thought prudent
to consult him. But the Emperor refused to be consulted. " It is your business to make the choice," he
said. " Choose a Bishop worthy of the office. To
such an one I will defer, and receive the instruction
necessary for salvation."

Failing to secure the Emperor's help the Bishops
fixed a day for the election. They assembled in the apse
of one of the basilicas of Milan, and were, I suppose,
concealed from the view of the nave by the altar and
surrounding structure. The nave was packed with a tur-
bulent mob. It is curious to remember that the confirmation of Dr. Ingram, Bishop of London, was conducted
under similar circumstances. I was present at it in Bow
Church, when Mr. Kensit made an attack upon the
Bishop and was only saved from the fury of the Catholic
crowd by the police. On that occasion Bow Church
rang with angry shouts from the swaying, dangerously
excited throng.

The Basilica, where the election took place, perished
long ago. The oldest churches in Milan are S. Ambrogio,
which St. Ambrose built himself, and S. Lorenzo,
which is fashioned out of a hall of the Palace of Maximian.

They did not begin to build the present Duomo for a thousand years after St. Ambrose's day.

We can imagine the scene. The long lines of marble columns, the flat decorated roof, the mosaics rich in gold and colour. As the morning went on and no decision was reached, the excitement became dangerous, and the police sent word to the Prefect that bloodshed was imminent. Ambrose hastened from the prefecture and entered the basilica. Way was made for the idolized Prefect until he reached some commanding point, the steps of a pulpit probably, from which he could speak. A dead silence fell on the crowd as the Prefect's voice was heard. He spoke with his accustomed firmness, grace and sweetness. As he ended amid the silence which can be felt a baby broke the tension. It chirruped the two words that had been falling persistently on baby ears, " Ambrose! Bishop ! "

How well we can see it all. The crowd titters, " Oh! do listen to that child ! " Then again, " Ambrose! Bishop ! " The people look at each other. " Well, and why not ? What better bishop could there be ? " A third time the baby voice, "Ambrose, Bishop ! "

" By Heaven ! it is an inspiration. It is an angel speaking through the child. Yes, it shall be. Ambrose shall be Bishop ! Ambrose shall be Bishop ! "

Aroused and indignant the Prefect gesticulated his protests against the tumult. " How insane crowds are ! " he said. " What a disgusting position to find oneself in ! " But the din went on, and the frightened Bishops in the apse broke off their consultations, and began to discuss the new situation in excited tones. Ambrose a Bishop ! Well, that would indeed be a social uplifting for the Church! But then Ambrose, although a devout believer, had never entered the Catholic Church. Meanwhile the Prefect, in rapidly-growing anxiety, perplexity and trouble had gone to the law courts followed by a swelling crowd, yelling ceaselessly, "Ambrose is our Bishop." The idea spread throughout the city. The Prefect was a great man of affairs, and he knew that a genuine popular movement had arisen, and one it would be hard to withstand.

But what a horrible fate, what a nightmare! He had mapped out his course in life, a course too common in great families of those days. He would lead as decent and edifying a life as he could, and then on his deathbed he would receive the sacrament of baptism, which would remit all his sins, and he would go to God clad in his baptismal innocence.

But if this hideous idea were carried out he must forfeit all his earthly power and place. He must take the risks of living the Christian life in the middle of this miserable and naughty world, he must bear the appalling responsibility of the episcopate and live in a ceaseless atmosphere of theological conflict and moral struggle.

Remember, those were the days before the Bishop of Rome had arrogated to himself all responsibility for Christendom. Pope Damasus was a very strong man, primate of Christendom and successor of Peter, but he had not had much say in the ecclesiastical affairs of Milan. If you had told the Bishops of his day that he was the Infallible Vicar, and they his episcopal lieutenants, they would have expressed their amazement in vigorous terms. No, every Bishop then felt the full burden of the apostolic office as every bishop should.

And now Ambrose felt the lack of the sacramental grace he had seemed to do so well without. He was in the natural state. He was being called suddenly and violently into the supernatural by the way of the Cross, and the natural man rebelled. There are three stories of his struggle to avoid baptism and the episcopate. I tell you two with a strong query, the third I expect is true.

Ambrose was unfortunate in his biographer, who had a love of marvels and that tendency to exaggeration which haunts the Catholic hagiographer. As in the case of St. Thomas of Canterbury, and, to a less extent, of St. Francis, there was a tendency to exaggerate the difference between the saint's later and earlier careers.

It is possible that this explains the two extraordinary stories which are told of Ambrose's struggle to avoid the bishopric. On the other hand, the standpoint of that day was so very different from ours that we are not good judges of what may or may not have happened.

It is said that Ambrose, who had ever been just and generous in his administration, now tried to disgust the people of Milan by being harsh and cruel. But the people were not deceived. " These sins be upon us," they said. It is also said that he who had ever been stainlessly pure in his life, tried to disgust the people by entertaining guests of bad character at the prefecture. But the people were not deceived, " These sins be upon us," they said.

Then the Prefect fled from the city. One dark thick night he slipped in disguise through the gates, and made for Pavia. You know the country round Milan, how flat and featureless it is, and how elaborately cultivated,

You remember the miles of tilled land; the rich, sticky soil showing in the furrows, and the miles of little mulberry trees. In those days England was forest and swamp, but the country round Milan was very much what it is to-day. The Prefect lost his way: at dawn he came, as he thought, to the gate of Pavia. But no, he had doubled back unconsciously, and he stood once more before the gate of Milan.

He was recognized and carried by force back to the house, where his loving subjects imprisoned him. The Bishops bowed to the popular choice; they elected Ambrose—as Ambrose said himself: " Rule was overridden by emotion."

The election was reported to the Emperor, and the Emperor gladly assented. Here was a bishop he could reverence indeed, and who would work with himself for the preservation of order. But when the Emperor's letter recognizing the new Bishop reached Milan, Ambrose was not there. He had slipped off again and was hiding in the country house of a friend. But the friend gave him up; he felt he could not resist the plain design of God. Then Ambrose yielded. The will of God was clear, the great sacrifice was being asked of him. He accepted the Cross at last and began the preparation for his baptism.

II

AMBROSE was about thirty-four when this tremendous convulsion occurred in his life. He was given no lengthy preparation for baptism, and only a week was allowed to elapse between his baptism and his elevation to the priesthood. On December 3rd, 374, at the end of the same year in which he had come to Milan as Viceroy of North Italy, Ambrose was consecrated and enthroned Bishop and Metropolitan of Milan.

Imagine Lord Irwin going out while a bachelor to India as viceroy; imagine him seized and forcibly made Metropolitan of India instead ; imagine him feeling it his duty to lay aside all wealth and comfort and to live an ascetical life like one of the Brahmin holy men. Imagine his getting such a grip on India in consequence that it was necessary during all the rest of his life to call him in constantly in the administration of Indian State affairs, and you get a situation more or less parallel to the story of St. Ambrose.

Now the tale that follows is a much more difficult tale to tell than that of St. Jerome. The life of St. Ambrose is so many-sided that it is easy to get a wrong impression of him. He combined the saint, the bishop and the man of affairs in a partly Pagan state. The story of St. Jerome is set in the history of the Roman Empire. The story of St. Ambrose is part of the history of the Roman Empire. There are the elements of the lives of three later saints in it—St. Anselm, St. Thomas of Canterbury, and his own glorious successor, St. Charles Borromeo.

I must begin by trying to picture the bishop who grew so steadily in Catholic sanctity. When I have tried to make you see him then I will tell you the story of how he defended the Faith and assisted in the affairs of the Empire.

Ambrose had always led a strictly moral, upright life based on Christian principle, and he was a well-read theologian; he began to teach and preach as soon as he was made bishop, but all his life he regretted the precipitancy of his election and consecration.

" Behold one," he says to himself, " whom the Church has not nurtured in her school, one who has not been subject to her yoke from his youth, who was accustomed to no psalms, no canticles, but the voice of the criers in the law courts, who now stands, but only by the grace of Christ, in the power of the priesthood and reclines among the faithful at the heavenly banquet. O Lord, keep, preserve the gift bestowed on him while yet he fled from Thee."

The day after the election of Ambrose he changed the mode of his life and abandoned the luxury of a great State official. His banking account he distributed among the poor ; he made a will leaving a life interest in his estate to the consecrated virgin, his sister Marcellina, but the money itself after her death to charity. He exchanged the dignity of the viceregal palace for a modest clergy house; the building ran along a bit of the inside of the city wall close to the spot where St. Ambrogio was afterwards built. The bishop lived there in community with the chief clergy of the diocese. They kept the fasts of the Church rigorously, and when they dined alone their meals were of a severe simplicity.

But Ambrose kept the paraphernalia of dignified dining ready in the background. When distinguished visitors came they were nobly entertained. He advised bishops to show not a reluctant but a generous hospitality. " The clergy," he says, " must not be vulgar or plebeian ; they ought not to have the manners and customs of the rougher class."

He remained a great gentleman, but his life from this moment was one of austerity, penance and hardship.

Dr. R. J. Campbell once wrote in the *Sunday Herald* that our world is much more like the world of Cicero than like the world of the days of St. Francis, and that he earnestly hoped that as a result of the war the world would again become more like the world of the days of St. Francis. I think he is right. As he says, we should without much difficulty understand men like Cicero and his contemporaries, but people like Francis would completely puzzle us. We should not be able to get near to them at all, so to speak. Their assumptions, ideals, beliefs, ways of expressing themselves are all widely different from ours. Dr. Campbell maintains that it is better to assimilate ourselves to the mental attitude of men like Francis than to that of men like Cicero.

Now take the case of St. Ambrose. English Christian civilization understands him and appreciates him while he remains the unbaptized prefect. Our English boys are trained to be like Ambrose the prefect, minus his singular knowledge of theology, but the moment Ambrose becomes a Catholic bishop he begins to become partly incomprehensible to English Christians. The majority of Italian bishops of the Renaissance, of French bishops before the French Revolution, and the majority of English bishops to-day would all agree in admiring Ambrose the prefect, but would secretly think that Ambrose the bishop had become less well-balanced and rather fanatical.

Let us try to see the ascetic bishop who lived in poverty with his clergy in the modest clergy-house.

We know that he had great distinction of face, bearing

and manner: he was singularly gentle and courteous, yet his enemies feared him, and those who did not agree with him respected him.

Augustine, while still unconverted, adored Ambrose; he was fond of dropping in at Bishop's House, but he did not always find the Bishop ready to talk to him. He complains somewhere that Ambrose used to sit reading in the loggia so absorbed that Augustine did not dare to interrupt him. Was Augustine rather trying, combative and talkative at this period? Probably. He was already a great man in his way. He was on the verge of becoming a Catholic, and his conversion would have been a valuable conquest for the Church. None of these things moved Ambrose. Evidently Augustine was piqued that Ambrose did not always find time for him, and I have no doubt that the little snub was good for Augustine. On the other hand, Ambrose was endlessly accessible to the poor and needy. He was besieged wherever he went by suppliants, and he was boundlessly tender and patient with them. This charity made no distinction between Christian and Pagan. Once an unfortunate Pagan was on the point of being executed for uttering some silly words against the young Emperor Gratian. Ambrose heard of it, and went straight to the Palace to get a pardon. Gratian, as we shall see presently, was devoted to Ambrose, but at this moment he was going out hunting, and there was a standing order that when he was going out hunting the Emperor must not be disturbed. Not even Ambrose could get admission. The Bishop went to the kennels, and went in with the hounds as one of the whips. In this way he got to Gratian, who, for the only time in his life, nearly lost his temper with Ambrose. When the Bishop urged that the man was merely a silly fool the Emperor turned away, saying sharply, " The man insulted me." "All the more reason for forgiving him," said Ambrose. There was something so enchanting in the Bishop's sweetness and audacity that Gratian's anger melted, and the man's life was saved.

At every available moment Ambrose studied, he was a very prolific writer, he wrote a theological treatise almost every year. His was not a great original mind, and he says he was not an orator, but no doubt he was accomplished in the art of speaking, he had had a legal training, and he had perfect command of himself. He preached almost every day; he was delightfully lucid and attractive, and all the great people of Milan came round the Bishop's pulpit. Among them came the Professor Augustine. " I used to hang intently on his words," says Augustine, " and I was enchanted by the charm of his style." Every day the Bishop said Mass, and the vigils and hours of prayer which he and his Presbyters kept were far beyond anything that we should think possible now in the West. He had a great devotion to the relics of the Saints, and loved to make pilgrimages to the tombs of the Martyrs.

The most intense grief of Ambrose's life was the death of his brother, which happened in the early years of his Episcopate. He had lived with Ambrose in the clergy-house, and had taken upon him as much of the secular work connected with the diocese as he could. Ambrose's love for him was most touching. After a while Satyrus went to Africa on business. On returning, the ship was wrecked, and he saved his life by his strong swimming. For a time it was thought he was lost, and there was great joy when the news of his safety reached Milan. He returned to die; the shock had undermined his health, and he breathed his last in the Bishop's arms. There was a great funeral, and the broken-hearted Bishop pronounced the oration on his adored brother. It is an extraordinary utterance. Ambrose takes all his people into the secrets of his grief. Picture the great basilica, the crowds, the dead form on the bier, and the figure of the Bishop standing before it. Imagine the tense silence which falls on all as the opening sounds were heard. They were like the sobbing of the violins at the opening of some great andante movement: " Oh, my brother, where shall I go ? Where shall I turn ? The ox seeks his fellow with whom he has borne the burden of the yoke and calls for him again and again. And I, brother, shall I forget you with whom I have borne the yoke of life ? I weep, but our Lord wept, too, at the tomb of Lazarus, who was His friend, and shall not I weep for him who is my brother?" Then he tells the story of his brother's death, and contrasts the Pagan gloom with the Christian hope, and at the end he comes to the bier and gazes on his brother's dead form for the last time.

" Why longer delay ? " he cries. " No doubt it is sweet to be able to gaze on that beauty, that grace, of which even death has not been able to rob his beloved features. But the hour is come, let us go to the grave. Go then, my brother, go before me to that last common dwelling of us both, which to me henceforward shall be dearer than any other. Here below we have had all in common ; there, also, may we not long be separated."

In those days people learnt oratory as to-day people

are trained to play musical instruments and to sing. St. Ambrose is said to have been the first Christian preacher who used Latin with oratorical effect. St. Basil, St. Gregory Nazianzen, St. John Chrysostom, all preached in Greek. Oratory had become very artificial, and Ambrose took great pains to adapt it to Catholic Christian use. " There must be no false ornament," he said, " the natural in you must be allowed to speak, and if the natural have faults they must not be crushed by artificial devices. Your voice must be properly modulated: you must not sometimes shout and sometimes whisper, and there must be nothing effeminate about your manner. Your voice must keep a certain form, rule and manly vigour."

Well, I have tried to show you something of the man, and now we must take up our tale and I must tell you how he ruled the Church, defended the Faith, and served the State.

The first act of St. Ambrose was to define his attitude in the Catholic battle against Arianism with unmistakable clearness. Dionysius, the Catholic Bishop of Milan, had been banished to Armenia, and had died a confessor for the Faith in a remote Armenian town. Ambrose's first act was to send an embassy to St. Basil, the greatest authority in the Church of the East, begging his help in recovering the body of Dionysius. The body was found, and St. Basil sent it with all honour to Milan and with it a letter of greeting.

" Let us give glory to God," writes St. Basil, " who calls out of each generation men worthy of His choice. He chose him who was the Prince of his people from among the shepherds. He chose Amos, a prophet

whom He filled with His Holy Spirit, from among the
goatherds, and in our own day He has sought in a royal
city one set over others to govern, and who by reason of
his lofty mind, his noble descent, his wealth and his
eloquence held the highest rank. Go therefore, O
man of God, thou chosen of the Lord from among
secular judges, go sit in the chair of the Apostles, fight the
good fight, and if thy people have suffered from the
infection of the Arian foolishness do thy best to heal
them."

There was a great scene in Milan. Ambrose and his
clergy in the midst of a great multitude solemnly received
the relics of the Catholic confessor Dionysius, and
renewed their vows of loyalty to the revelation of God
in His only-begotten Son, around the sacred tomb.

Ambrose was consecrated, as we have seen, on
December 3rd, 374, and the Emperor promised him he
should have a quiet Episcopate; but in the following
November the Emperor Valentinian I died suddenly,
near the modern Presburg, on the Danube, and great
troubles, secular and religious, began. The Emperor,
remember, was a Catholic; his brother Valens, the Eastern Emperor, was an Arian; and Valentinian's wife, the
Empress Justina, who was a hard, crafty type of woman,
had become a pervert to Arianism. Valentinian left
two sons. Gratian was a charming boy of seventeen,
the son of Valentinian's former wife Severa. Justina's boy, the little Valentinian, was only four years
of age.

Gratian, who had already been nominally associated
with his father in the Government, succeeded him
according to the usual custom; but the soldiers who sur-

rounded Valentinian at his death—he died of apoplexy while on a campaign against a German tribe—proclaimed the boy Valentinian Emperor. I suppose the army hoped for more power in this way. Gratian would have done well to fight the point, but he was devoted to his only brother, and he agreed that he should nominally share the throne with him. This, of course, meant that his step-mother, the Arian Empress Justina, became his reigning partner. Justina hated him as her child's rival, and hated the Catholics still more. At once the Arians plucked up courage and demanded to have their position in Milan recognized and legalized, and a Basilica secured to them. Here was a beautiful opportunity for unity at the price of principle, for the " live and let live " principle in matters of religion. Ambrose could have got a cheap popularity by saying that he was quite ready to let the Arians have some sort of *locus standi* side by side with the Catholics; but that was not Ambrose's way. He called upon the Emperor at once to forbid the scandal of this defiance of the authority of the Catholic Bishop. Gratian was a devout young Catholic, but he was not ready to take strong action. He shut up the Basilica which the Arians wanted to keep, and said he would look into the whole matter a little later. Then quite suddenly came the first great thrust against the fabric of the Empire, and the Goths came crashing in.

The Empire really went to pieces by becoming too big for a properly co-ordinated government. It had to be divided for practical purposes, and dividing the Empire was like cutting Samson's hair—the power of the charm seemed to disappear. It lost its quasi-divinity in losing its unity. Valentinian had made his brother Valens Emperor of the East, with his capital at Constantinople. Valens was a fanatical Arian; he cared for nothing in the world so much as promoting the Arian cause, and his reign was bloody and persecuting, and his preoccupation with the promulgation of heresy was really the immediate cause of the Empire's downfall. He did not give sufficient attention to the signs of the times, and he fell into a fatal mistake in respect to the Goths.

For centuries the Yellow Peril had been threatening the Empire. The Huns, a great and warlike Tartar nation, had failed to conquer China, and failing to settle eastward had gone on rolling west. They had conquered the predecessors of the Don Cossacks and had joined forces with them, and together the Alani and the Huns had entered Roumania, and set themselves to conquer the Goths, who then inhabited it. The Goths, the inhabitants of Roumania, were by far the strongest of the nations on the other side of the Empire's border, and the Empire had thought it best to take up a conciliatory position towards them. It had a kind of commercial treaty with them. The Goths had a rude civilization of their own, and their Constitution was a Monarchy. They were most of them Christians, and one of them, Ulfilas, had become a bishop. Their Christianity was of a naive, uninstructed sort, very much like that of the ancient British Church.

This nation, the most formidable and respectable of the Barbarian nations, being threatened by the Huns on the north, began to look south across the Danube into the portions of the Empire nearest to them, the portions which are now Bulgaria and European Turkey.

They decided to abandon Roumania and migrate into Bulgaria and European Turkey. They preferred coming into the unity of the Empire to being conquered by the Huns.

Of course a great Barbarian invasion had been haunting the Roman mind for years, as for years German aggression haunted the mind of modern Europe. The authorities had been watching the approach of the Huns, and hoping that the Goths would prove a strong breakwater. Now suddenly the Goths sent a deputation to Constantinople with Bishop Ulfilas at its head. The deputation proposed that the whole nation should evacuate Roumania and enter the Empire, promising to keep to any area delimited by the Imperial Authority, and to be loyal and faithful subjects. It was a distracting problem. The stronger councillors told the Emperor that this must be resisted by force, that it was opening the door of the fold to let the wolf in; others said that defence was impossible, that the Goths were too strong and could force the passage of the Danube.

Valens took the middle course of the weak man. He decided that the Goths should be let in, but on two conditions—they must lay down their arms and enter the Empire defenceless, and they must abandon their Catholicism and accept the Arian creed. The Emperor really cared more about the conversion of a whole nation to Arianism than he did about his more practical condition. Ulfilas was too simple and uninstructed to object seriously to the Arian creed. " I don't see," he said why we should not do what the Emperor asks ; these minutiæ of theology are not very important at the crisis of our nation's fate ; they must not be allowed to count one way or the other. Who could maintain a theological controversy in the hour of our nation's peril ? " You observe that the good old Ulfilas talked very much like the sort of English layman who is regarded as a pillar of the Establishment. I think the Goths were quite honest and became Arians because they really thought it did not matter.

But giving up their arms was quite another thing. It was understood that they should do so, but it was impossible to carry out the promise—you cannot take his dirk and claymore away from a Highlander, and a Goth's sword belonged to him as much as his trousers and tunic did ; and when the whole nation surged over like a tidal wave into the Empire it did not leave its swords behind. No arbitrarily-created limits stopped it. When the imperial police tried to regulate the Gothic movement the Goths cried that they were betrayed and flung themselves into fighting array. A great panic seized the inhabitants of the invaded province: they fled like the Russian peasants before the Germans. If you want to know what happened, read that appalling description of the events of 1915 on the Russian front, *The Way of the Cross*, by Doroshevitch.

Valens sent to Gratian for help, and the young Emperor was torn asunder by divided counsels. If he marched eastward against the Goths how could he be sure that the Franks would not fling themselves into the Empire across the Rhine ? In the end Gratian sent an army against the Goths and promised to send another army in the spring. Meanwhile he felt he must prepare himself for the religious controversy which must ensue if he entered deeply into Eastern politics, and in his anxiety the boy turned to Ambrose. This was the beginning of his devoted friendship with the great Bishop.

Ambrose was profoundly moved by the evils of the Gothic invasion; as a Roman, he felt the outrage to the Empire's sacred soil; as a Catholic he felt the menace to be the menace of heresy, and in the whole movement he saw heresy being punished by heresy. He gave Gratian a great treatise on the Divinity of our Lord. "When the faith is assailed," he cried, "nothing is safe. Arise now, therefore, O Lord God, and unfurl Thy standard. Not now shall the eagles lead our standards, but Thy Name, O Lord Jesus, which our armies invoke, and Thy Cross, which goes before them." It was as a crusade that Ambrose bade Gratian's army go forth. But it went too late. At Adrianople the Imperial forces had been overwhelmingly beaten by the Goths. The road to Byzantium lay open, pillage, famine and pestilence devastated the Eastern Empire. At any moment the conquerors might enter Italy. Trenches were dug and the Tyrolese gorges were blocked by felled pine trees. "These are the last days," cried Ambrose. "The world is set to its fall, and we behold the signs of its dissolution." Refugees poured in, and Ambrose gave himself to the work we learnt to do in the war. The prisoners were sold by the Goths as slaves. Ambrose had no money left, but he took the gold vessels from the churches and broke them up to ransom the captives. "If the Blood of Christ redeemed their souls," he said, "should not the vessels which hold that Blood be used to redeem their bodies?"

III

THE battle of Adrianople, the first great success won by barbarians against the Empire, brought to it a compensating advantage in the death of the Emperor Valens. It was a terrible death. He was forsaken, lying wounded in a hut, when the flight of the Imperial troops became general, and the hut and Valens within it were destroyed by fire.

Ultimately the Gothic attack got dissipated over the huge spaces of the Empire, and was brought to a standstill, while a new Emperor was sent to the invaded East who was quite capable of dealing with the situation. Theodosius, to whom the young Emperor Gratian now offered the sceptre of the East, was by birth a Spaniard but by training a Briton. His father, a noted general under Valentinian, had saved London once in a great attack upon it. Here Theodosius learnt the art of soldiering, and he may very well have drilled his troops upon the ground on which stands the Church of All Saints, Margaret Street. In Britain he was appointed to high command, and it was in Britain that he gained the reputation which led him to the throne. His father had fallen under suspicion, and had been put to death by Valentinian, and the son was living in retirement on the family estates at Cauca, in Spain, when Gratian summoned him to deal with the situation in the East, and offered him the crown. It was with great difficulty that Theodosius was persuaded to emerge from obscurity, and his accession was the greatest blessing to the Church. It was Theodosius who secured the triumph of Catholicism in the East. He ascended the throne a Catholic in sympathy, but unbaptized. Gratian had made his task easy for him by repealing all the anti-Catholic measures of Valens, but it was the happy accident of a very serious illness which brought Theodosius to the point of baptism. He established his Court at Thessalonica because Salonica is the best point from which to deal with the parts overrun by the Goths—Serbia, Bulgaria and Roumania. But at this supreme moment the new Emperor was brought near to death by illness. Ascholius, Bishop of Thessalonica, a devout Catholic and a bosom friend of St. Ambrose, prepared him for baptism and gave him the sacraments, and henceforth Theodosius was a great Christian knight sworn to promote and defend the Catholic cause. How dramatically he enters later into the story of Ambrose you all remember.

Now we return to St. Ambrose himself. The Gothic invasion had given Catholic Christianity an opportunity of showing itself in its true light; it appeared then, as it appeared to us all in the Great War, the only religion which can succour mankind in its extremity, and Ambrose embodied it. He was raised up by God to be the typical Catholic Christian figure. As such he entirely captivated the charming young Emperor Gratian. At the end of the Eastern campaign it was desirable that the Emperor should go far west and establish his Court for a time at Treves, so as to make the Imperial power felt in that region. To Treves he summoned Ambrose in order that Ambrose might continue to train him in the Catholic Religion, and Ambrose refused to go. No, he was Bishop of Milan, he could not leave his diocese and form part of the Imperial entourage at Treves.

" If," he wrote, " I have not come into the presence

of your clemency, pious Emperor, it is not from lack of affection ; discretion has retained me. But I have been present with you unceasingly in prayer and aspiration, the manner best becoming a priest to render you what is due to you."

You appreciate the true greatness of this answer of Ambrose, and so did the Emperor. Later on he moved the Court to Milan, and remained there, very largely that he might have the companionship and advice of the Bishop.

St. Ambrose stood upon the Mount of the Temptation while Satan spread before him the kingdoms of the world. "All these things will I give thee," said Satan, " if thou wilt fall down and worship me." Ambrose's answer is apparent in the inflexible character of his attitude through the prosperity of these years and the adversity of those that followed. While Gratian lived, Ambrose was to a large extent Emperor of the West. When the Emperor was absent on military expeditions, Ambrose entered his cabinet with a latchkey; all the while he was the ascetic Bishop living plainly with his clergy, bent on fasting and prayer; all his old power as consul was at the service of the Empire, but this reversion to former tasks was never at the expense of his position and work as the greatest Catholic Bishop of those times in the West.

There is one picturesque incident of the reign of Ambrose. The Roman Senate remained largely Pagan —the majority, that is to say, were Pagan in the sense in which the majority of the present House of Commons are Christians ; in the sense that they did not profess any other religion. In the Hall of the Senate stood the altar of the goddess of victory, and the Pagan senators valued this altar very much. It stood to them for the good old order of things which this pestilent Catholicism had so largely superseded. They believed in the goddess of victory very much as the majority of the English believe in St. George to-day, and were ready to shout "goddess of victory" before Catholics very much as our statesmen might shout "St. George and Merry England" before a foreign foe. The Christian senators tolerated the presence of the altar on the plea that it now only symbolized an idea, like our Britannia. But one day the senators entered the senate hall to find the altar of victory gone. The feeling was most violent. The Christian senators were afraid to intervene. They told Pope Damasus what had happened, and asked him to explain to the Emperor that it was not advisable that the Christians of Rome should appear in the matter.

Consequently the embassy which arrived at Milan to demand the restoration of the altar of victory could claim to represent a unanimous voice. No Christian voice had been raised against it. But at Milan the ambassadors were met by impenetrable silence. They could get no audience of Gratian, and soon afterwards the removal of the altar was followed by the seizure of its endowments and the suppression of its priests and vestals. Wicked men, said the Senate, had brought about this outrage against the dignity of Rome, but everyone knew who had done it. It was Ambrose.

But far more dangerous to the Faith than dying Paganism was the worldly and semi-pagan Arianism. Arianism, thanks to Theodosius and St. Gregory Nazianzen in the East, and to Gratian and St. Ambrose in the West, was for the moment in a bad way, and its bitterness was extreme. The Empress Justina was its champion, and in the little opposition court, which she had gathered round the young Valentinian II at Sirmium, Arianism reigned supreme. In 380 Ambrose had to go there to consecrate a new Catholic Bishop. The Arians filled the church and gave him an outrageous reception. Amid the yells and hoots an Arian nun, with the enthusiasm of a Jenny Geddes, flung herself on the Bishop of Milan and tried forcibly to prevent him from taking his seat in the episcopal chair.

Ambrose stood quite still, and then, in an awful tone, he said to the wild woman, " Touch me not, I am a priest, however unworthy, and against a priest you have no right to stretch out your hand. Beware, lest God punish you with some great misfortune." This incident did more to destroy Arianism than anything else, for by a terrible coincidence the nun died a few days afterwards.

Next year the remaining Arian bishops were tried and deposed at the Synod of Aquileia, of which Ambrose was the ruling spirit. The Synod wrote a stirring letter against Arianism to the three Emperors, and Justina never forgave the language in which the religion she was teaching her boy of ten, Valentinian II, was denounced in the letter addressed to him.

In the next year, 382, Ambrose went to Rome for the first time for eight years. He went there to attend that ineffective Roman Council we heard of in the story of St. Jerome, which met to examine the decisions of the Œcumenical Council of Constantinople. He had a tremendous reception in Rome. He was received as

Father John of Kronstadt used to be received in Russia. There was great belief in the miraculous power of his prayers, and the sick and the poor crowded round him. In the home of his youth he found the last of his nearest and dearest awaiting him, the consecrated virgin Marcellina. His mother had died when he could not be with her, and now, too, his brother was gone. It was a moment of intense emotion, and the brother and sister cried and laughed as she knelt before him, and he, recalling the scene of long ago, held out his hands for her to kiss.

" I told you you would have to come to it," he said; " you are not going to refuse now to kiss the bishop's hands."

But the enthusiasm of the Catholics deepened the hostility of the enemies of Ambrose. He was kept eight months in Rome by the affairs of the Church, and during this time there came a breakdown of the food supply and the city suffered from famine. It was easy to say famine had fallen on the city because the man who had dethroned the goddess of victory was living in it, and this was freely said. But Ambrose paid no heed. Calmly he organized relief, giving most generously himself and getting great sums from his Catholic friends. The Church's charity was a bloodless victory, and the blessings of the people followed the Bishop when he returned to his diocese.

He returned to deep personal sorrow—to find all his hopes of serving the State overturned. There had been a revolt in the army of Gaul. The soldiers had made one of their generals, Maximus, their Emperor. They had carried all the province with them, and when Gratian had hurried to the scene only the Governor of Lyons offered him allegiance. And it was in treachery he did it: that first night Gratian was murdered while at supper in the governor's house, crying aloud for Ambrose as he died.

It was an appalling grief and shock for Ambrose, and as he sat stunned beneath it, he remembered that now the Arian Empress Justina, mother of the child Valentinian, was virtually Empress of the West, and that the Arians and Pagans were rejoicing at his downfall.

But the first move of the Empress was dramatic and unexpected. When she arrived at Milan she went straight to the Bishop's modest house, taking her boy with her. She entered the Bishop's presence leading the boy by the hand, and then she lifted him up and laid the little Emperor in the Bishop's arms.

"Bishop," she said, "protect my little child." Justina was playing a deep game. She saw that her boy's only chance lay in a partition of the Western Empire. Maximus must be prevented from crossing the Alps. He must be offered Gaul, Spain and Great Britain, on the undertaking that he would not invade Italy and the Danube provinces, and the Empress knew that there was only one man in the Empire sufficiently strong, courageous, unselfish and single-minded to penetrate the lines of the enemy and conduct the negotiations, and that man was the Bishop of Milan.

Ambrose went at once. It was late in the year, the season was severe, but he and his colleague, Count Bauto, at once proceeded to make the passage of the Alps and enter the enemy's country. At Mainz they met a similar embassy going the other way, for Maximus had realized that he had a more formidable force to reckon with than the boy Valentinian and his mother. There was also the great Theodosius, who, if he espoused their cause, might deprive Maximus of all he had gained. So Maximus was ready to acquiesce in a partition of the Empire. But he was rude and dilatory, he treated Ambrose roughly and discourteously, and the cold winter months which the Bishop spent in the usurper's province, while Justina played skilfully with his ambassador and at the same time fortified the passes of the Alps, must have been some of the most irksome in Ambrose's life.

When all was adjusted Ambrose returned to face some of the greatest troubles of his career. In his absence a strong and very natural effort had been made by the Pagans to restore the altar of victory in the Senate House. Of course the calamities which had recently befallen the Empire were due to the insult done to the tutelary deity of Rome! I daresay belief in the goddess of victory obtained some renascence through the coincidence, and now the younger Symmachus, the Prefect of Rome, noble son of a noble father, sent a very impressive petition for the restoration of the altar to Justina and young Valentinian. Towards its close Rome herself addressed the Emperors Western and Eastern.

" Excellent Princes," cried the great city, " Fathers of our country, have respect for the old age I have arrived at under this sacred law. Leave me my ancient solemnities. I have no cause to depart from them. Leave me free to live in the manner that pleases me, and in the way to which I am accustomed. This is the worship which drove Hannibal from my ramparts, the Gauls from my capital. Have I lived so long to come at last to this dishonouring change ? We ask for peace for the gods of our fathers. No doubt it is just to confess that there is but one Being whom all should worship, for all of us look upon the same stars, all are covered by one heaven, all dwell in one world. But of what matter is the manner in which each seeks for truth ? There must be more than one road to reach the great mystery of Nature."

Fortunately Ambrose returned while this letter was still under debate by the authorities at Milan. They did not think it wise to mention it to him, but he heard of it and sent a peremptory message to the Emperor, demanding to see it. If it had been a matter concerning military affairs it would have been addressed to the generals. This concerned religion. Very well, in Milan the Bishop of Milan was the proper person to consult. It was impossible to refuse the Bishop's request. The petition was handed over to him and he tore its argument to shreds in a burning reply. He, too, speaks in the name of Rome. " Rome did not tell you to say what you have said," he cries ; " other is her language. Why, she asks, do you daily come with blood, offering many flocks with useless sacrifice ? Not in the quivering entrails of victims is victory to be found, but in the valour of armed men. By no other science have I conquered the world. Camillus, armed, drove the Gauls over the Tarpeian Rock, and tore down their standard floating over the capital. Courage overcame those whom the gods had not repulsed. Why do you hold up my ancestors to me ? The worship Nero practised is hateful to me. I regret my error in the past, and I am not ashamed in my old age to change with a changing world. It is never too late to learn. There is no shame in passing over from one party to another which is better. Formerly I had this in common with the barbarian nations—I knew not God."

Then Ambrose appeals to Symmachus and his friends. " Come and join us in the heavenly army. In it we fight ; in it we live. Learn the mysteries of Nature from God, who created Nature, not from man, who knows nothing about it himself. Whom should I believe about God more than God Himself ? How am I to believe you, who yourselves tell me you know not what you worship ? You tell me there must be more than one road to the knowledge of the mystery of Nature. What you know not God has taught us. What you think to discover we, through the wisdom and truth of God, have learnt. Between our thought and yours, therefore, there is nothing in common. You ask the Emperors to give your gods peace. We ask God to give our Emperors peace."

The Emperor's decision was given in Council. The Roman petition and Ambrose's rejoinder were both read in his presence. The rejoinder of Ambrose carried the day, the Council was strongly affected by it, and the young Valentinian gave his decision in words so admirably chosen that one cannot help suspecting they were chosen for him.

" I cannot undo what my brother has done," he said. " I am told my father did not take away the altar, but neither was he asked to put the altar back. I imitate him, therefore, in changing nothing that was done before my time."

So the goddess lost her throne and the enemies of Ambrose became more dangerous. It was clear that for the dying Paganism this strong new faith was too much, and so a most determined effort was now made to weaken the Church, and the Arians were encouraged to fight the great Bishop on his own ground at Milan.

IV

At the end of the last chapter we watched St. Ambrose vanquishing the goddess of victory, and by banishing her altar for ever from the Roman Senate House, administering its death-blow to the old religion of the Roman State. But Paganism did not yet know that it was beaten, and now it attempted to weaken the Church by aiding the Arian cause, and encouraging the Arians to fight the great Bishop on his own ground at Milan.

When, on the death of Gratian, the Empress Mother came to Milan from Sirmium, she brought a train of Arians with her, all hoping to advance their cause under the new *régime*. With them came a bishop, a Goth by birth, to whom, in memory of St. Ambrose's Arian predecessor at Milan, the name Auxentius had been given. This little device of producing another Arian Bishop Auxentius at Milan stimulated the enthusiasm of the Milanese Arians; it sounded as if the good old Arian times were coming back.

But the Catholic Church, under the most formidable and immovable of Bishops, was in complete possession of Milan. No church was available for Arian worship, and the Empress directed that a big building, which was part of the palace stables, should be converted into a chapel. St. Ambrose, commenting on this afterwards, remarked very naughtily that it ought to have suited the congregation very well. The Goths were so accustomed to living in their chariots that it would make them feel at home to have chariots all round them in church.

But the Arian body naturally grew under the more favourable conditions of the new reign, and it was privately suggested to them that if they petitioned the State to grant them a basilica the request would not be refused. The young Valentinian, who had acted so well in the matter of the altar of victory, could not be expected to act in this matter as a convinced Catholic. He behaved like Dr. Liddon's moderately good Churchman, whom he compared to the moderately good egg. "Bishop Ambrose is too extreme for me," was what he said in effect. "Christian charity requires a moderation and toleration greater than his. I really must insist on a dignified church being assigned to those who, with me, hold moderate opinions." For remember, that was what Arian Christianity claimed to be. It claimed to be moderate, primitive and strictly scriptural; its objection to the word *Homoousion* was that it went further than the Bible.

So they determined to give one of St. Ambrose's Catholic basilicas to Auxentius, and then with some trepidation proceeded to tell St. Ambrose of their decision. He was summoned to the palace.

I fancy that matters had been getting strained between Church and State for some time, because the news that Ambrose had been summoned to a private audience spread like wildfire through the city. The impression got about that his life was in danger. When Ambrose reached

the palace he found the boy Emperor, a youthful King
Edward VI, surrounded by his principal officers of
State. In a few abrupt words the boy repeated his
lesson: the Bishop was to vacate the Portian basilica.
The Portian basilica stood outside the gate: it was an
old church, of late superseded by a new and bigger one
inside the city. " I have no right to give up the basilica
to you," said the Bishop, " and you have no right to
take it. You would not seize the home of a private
citizen, and yet you think you may seize the House of
God."

" But," said the Emperor, " I have a right to a basilica
to practise my religion in."

" No," said the Bishop, " you have not. Union with
Christ which is not legitimate union is adultery. You
should have nothing to do with adultery."

At this there was very naturally a chorus of protest
from the courtiers, but at the same moment, from all
sides, there came into the palace a sound which Roman
Emperors had reason to fear. The people had risen and
were coming to the rescue of Ambrose. They surrounded the palace, demanding the Bishop. It was
eagerly explained to them that the Bishop was perfectly
safe, that they were quite mistaken, and that the matter
at issue was quite a trifling one. It was merely a question
of ceding one of the churches to the Arians. But to this
the Catholic crowd shouted, " Then we stay to defend
that basilica. Never shall it be given up." At last an
officer told the crowd that he had orders to disperse it
by force.

" Strike us if you will," shouted the crowd. " We
are all ready to die for the Faith of Jesus Christ."

The authorities looked very anxious, and the Empress Mother trembled. She saw herself and the boy Valentinian perishing as so many of their predecessors had perished. She implored Ambrose to go out and satisfy the people by showing himself to them.

" And what shall I say to them ? " said the Bishop.

" Tell them that the basilica will not be taken."

Ambrose told them, and the crowd went rejoicing home, and peace reigned once more through the city.

But in the calm the resentment of the court against the Bishop blazed out afresh. " The fact is," said the authorities, "Ambrose worked up that rising. It was a stage crowd raised by the Bishop and manipulated by him to secure his own ends. We have been duped."

And so almost at once high officials went to the Bishop's house, bearing an Imperial order. The Bishop was to vacate not only the Portian basilica but also the great basilica near his house. "And," said the officials, " this time he is to see that there is no rising."

" My answer," said the Bishop, " is the answer I gave at the palace to the Emperor, and I have nothing more to say."

This happened on Friday in Passion Week. The Bishop went on with his ordinary life, his prayers, his studies, his ministrations, quite unmoved, and on Palm Sunday morning he went to the great basilica to pontificate at the solemn Mass of Palm Sunday. The basilica was crowded, and popular feeling, it was evident, ran very high.

The Bishop was actually ascending the altar steps when the Prefect of the Prætorium went up to him.

He proposed a compromise: "If you will give up the small basilica," he said, "I will use the utmost of my power to get the authorities to leave this church, which after all is the important church, in your hands."

"Ambrose," cried the people, who suspected that the whispered consultation meant mischief, "give nothing up, nothing at all."

Ambrose ascended to the altar and began the Mass. As Mass went on news came to the Bishop that the Treasury officials had taken possession of the Portian basilica and had put the curtains up on either side the principal doors, which was the sign that the building had been taken for Imperial purposes; also that the Catholics were rising throughout the city, that a collision with the troops was imminent at the Portian basilica, and that a Catholic mob had laid hold of an Arian presbyter, and that his life was in danger.

When he heard that there was a fear that the Catholics would do violence to an Arian, St. Ambrose burst into a torrent of tears. He stopped the Mass for a moment and sent priests and deacons to rescue the man. Then, with tears streaming down his face, he went on with the service. Writing of it afterwards, he says: "I wept bitterly, and during the holy oblation I prayed to God so to order events that not a single drop of blood should be shed in the name of the Church, but that it should be rather mine that was shed for the salvation not only of the people but also of these impious men themselves. When I heard that armed men were to be sent to seize the basilica I feared some massacre might turn to the ruin of the city and I prayed to God that I might not survive the ruin of such a town, ruin that might become perhaps that of the whole of Italy."

When the Mass was over, St. Ambrose went on with the ordinary duties of the day and gave the final instructions to the catechumens who were to receive baptism on Easter Eve. It was a strange Holy Week. The city was on the verge of rebellion; the feeling of the army was largely on the Catholic side. Gothic Arian regiments had to be used. The minor Imperial officials scarcely dared show themselves; but the Government announced that since the merchants and tradesmen were acting disloyally severe financial penalties would be inflicted on them. They made a magnificent retort. " We care little if we are doubly or trebly taxed so long as we can uphold the Faith." It was supposed by everyone that St. Ambrose would be seized, but he took no measures for safety. He went on with his prayers and sermons and work as though there was no disturbance in the air.

In the middle of Holy Week the Bishop was told that the Arian Bishop would celebrate in the newly-acquired basilica on Easter Day, and that the Emperor would assist, surrounded by the State officials. St. Ambrose's reply was to issue a warning that any Catholic who accompanied the Emperor would be *ipso facto* excommunicate. He issued this pastoral letter just before going into the pulpit to preach. His sermon was a calm exposition of a bit of the Book of Job, which formed a part of the office for the day. While he was preaching the tramp of soldiery was heard approaching the church. The congregation was seized with panic, the women shrieked. They thought that the Bishop was about to

117

be seized, and that they would be scattered or massacred. The soldiers streamed into the building, saying quietly, " We have come to pray." The army, in fact, had declared for Ambrose. " If the Emperor is going to join the Catholics," they said, " we shall follow him, but if not we shall go and pray with Ambrose." And the Emperor's advisers dared no more. The people, all jubilant, tore down the Imperial hangings from the Portian basilica and children marched about Milan dressed up in the fragments.

They wished to carry Ambrose in triumph, but Ambrose would have no demonstration. To avoid it he did not go back to his house, but spent the following night in the church. During the rest of Holy Week popular feeling remained in a dangerously excited state, and on Easter Day the Catholic triumph was complete. Imprisoned Catholics were liberated, the money fines were remitted, and any claim on the basilicas was given up.

But naturally the chagrin of the Emperor and his advisers was extreme. One of the Imperial Chamberlains turned furiously on the Bishop when he next met him. " You bring the Emperor into contempt," he cried. " I swear I will stand you no longer. I will have your head off."

" And if you get me beheaded," said Ambrose, " I shall only die as a Catholic bishop should, and you will only act as palace eunuchs are in the habit of acting."

St. Paul and St. Thomas of Canterbury would both have made the same sort of retort.

For nearly a year after this no further effort was made by the Arians. When they moved again it was both

violently and foolishly. In Lent, 386, the Empress
Mother got a properly-sanctioned Imperial decree drawn
up and promulgated, which practically disestablished the
religion of the majority, Catholicism, and established the
religion of the Arian minority. The law first of all gave
full and entire liberty of assembly to all who professed
Arianism according to the formula of the Council of
Rimini. The creed of Rimini was declared to be the
true faith in conformity with the decrees of the whole
Church, which had there assembled, which would continue to exist until the end of time, and which then had
included all who since had separated from it. "As for
those others," said the decree, meaning the Catholics,
" if they still are allowed to assemble, it is only by virtue
of the Emperor's good pleasure."

And it concluded thus: "As for those who think that
they alone have the right to assemble, let it be known
to them that should they attempt to stir up any disturbance in hindrance of the execution of these laws of our
Serenity, they will be considered seditious persons,
disturbers of the Church, guilty of the crime of high
treason, and shall pay the penalty of their faults with
their heads. The same penalty will also be accorded to
those who by their prayers either in secret or in any
private place shall oppose our injunction."

So by a stroke of the pen St. Ambrose was deprived
of his legal status and outlawed, with his head as the
penalty for any disobedience. Every eye was turned
on him. What did he do ? Nothing whatever. He
did not take the smallest notice of the decree. He made
no alteration in his usual habits, and moved about Milan
just as usual. His business often took him past the

palace gates. He was followed and met by numbers who sought to kiss the hem of his robe. No hand was raised against him, and he gives the reason in memorable words: " The prayers of the poor," he said, " were my defence."

But there were all sorts of fearful rumours current among the faithful. Assassins had been hired, and at some unexpected moment they would strike. He was to be seized, flung into a covered carriage, and carried off into hidden captivity. Meanwhile the authorities suggested to him privately that they wished to act with leniency. " Go away from Milan," they said. " We do not wish to injure you. Go, and let those who agree with you follow; form a Catholic settlement elsewhere. What is impossible is that you should remain here flouting the Emperor to his face."

" Dear me," said Ambrose dryly, " this is a mild way of carrying out the terrific edict against the Catholics, and I do not intend to budge an inch."

Again Palm Sunday came round, and the Bishop proceeded as was customary to the great basilica to perform the ceremonies of the day. But the faithful had meanwhile been laying plans unknown to the Bishop, and when at the end of Mass he prepared to return to Bishop's House he found his way barred. The Catholic laity had converted the great basilica into an armed fortress, and they proposed to keep the Bishop safe there until the danger was past. There were big cloisters and buildings attached to the basilica.

There would have been no real difficulty in storming the place and taking it, but that the Imperial authorities did not dare to do. They encircled the great basilica with a cordon of soldiers, and bade them remain there until the people got tired and came out. But the people did not come out ; day after day the great multitude remained locked up in the church, with the Bishop in the midst of them. The Bishop was really being kept against his will. He was much touched by his people's care for him, and I suspect that he felt that the hand of God was controlling the whole matter, and that something was to come out of all this which he could not foresee. But he chided the people gently. " You are really troubling yourselves in vain in all this," he said. " Everything will be as God wills."

Days and nights passed. The times when the office was not being said hung heavily. No one would leave yet everyone grew restless, and then a great inspiration came to St. Ambrose. He had long wished to improve the music of the Church, which was very poor and rough. He had composed a good many hymns, and it struck him that this was an opportunity to teach the Milanese to sing in the effective Oriental way. The Orientals sang antiphonally, but antiphonal singing had not yet been introduced into the West. Ambrose seized upon this opportunity to introduce it, and so the siege became an enormous choir practice. The Bishop got two choirs, a choir of men and a choir of women, to answer one another. These strange sounds penetrated to the soldiers who encircled the church. They had never heard the alternate sounds of men's and treble choirs responding to one another before, and they decided that Ambrose was practising magical incantations in the church and weaving spells against his enemies.

" Well," said the Bishop afterwards, with a smile,

" there was some truth in that; those hymns worked wonders." There is no doubt that it was the siege of the great basilica which brought most of St. Ambrose's hymns into the services of the Church—for example, the office hymn of Eastertide. Do not forget the occasion when, in all probability, it was first heard. Think of the great basilica packed with sleepless, weary-eyed, hungry people. Think of the beginning of the Mass of Easter under these weird and terrible circumstances, and then the answering choirs of men and women :

> The Lamb's high banquet called to share,
> Arrayed in garments white and fair,
> The Red Sea past we fain would sing
> To Jesus our triumphant King.

What point the siege of the basilica gives to the verse:

> O all-sufficient Sacrifice,
> Beneath Thee Hell defeated lies,
> Thy captive people are set free
> And crowns of life restored by Thee.

Among other well-known hymns which were then perhaps sung for the first time are the hymns for the canonical hours, such as: "Come, Holy Ghost, who ever One, O God of truth, O Lord of might, O God of all the strength and power, Before the ending of the day . . ." and perhaps, too, the office hymn of apostles: " The Eternal Gifts of Christ the King."

This extraordinary condition of things lasted over Easter. Then the authorities made overtures of reconciliation. The Emperor proposed that Ambrose should meet Auxentius, the Arian bishop, in the state courts and that their case should be decided by arbiters. The Emperor made one stipulation, the arbiters were not to be ecclesiastics but laymen. Auxentius had already made his choice of laymen.

The weakness of the whole proposal was absurd. According to the recent Act, Ambrose ought to be beheaded. Ambrose wrote the Emperor a spirited reply. "Where," he asks, "have you ever heard of bishops allowing laymen to be their judges? Are laymen henceforth to make the laws of the Church? When you are older you will see what you yourself think of a bishop who consents to such a thing. Permit me," he says, "to decline to attend your consistory. It is a place I only once found my way to, and then I went there in your interest."

When St. Ambrose had finished his letter he entered the great basilica and sat himself on the episcopal throne of Milan. From the throne he told the Church what he had suffered in the past year and was still suffering. "I give my allegiance to the Emperor," he said, "but I do not give way to him." And he closed the whole controversy in historical words, words which are a milestone in Church history : "The Emperor is in the Church, not over it."

I need not remind you all that for seventy years we have been fighting this battle over again with the English State, and that our answer to those who would abolish Catholic usage on the authority of secular state tribunals is the answer of St. Ambrose. "We give our allegiance to the State, but we do not in this give way to it. The King is in the Church, not over it."

And what had God meant by that strange occupation

of the basilica for so long by the Catholics ? What good had come of it ? At least this: in the basilica during all that time there knelt and prayed an elderly woman who had come all the way from Africa to Milan in the hope of saving her wayward son, and outside, without doubt, coming back and back, strolling restlessly in and out among the soldiery, pausing in the depths of the night to listen to that strange singing, might have been seen a brilliant, moody, ill-controlled, unhappy man, a well-known Theosophist, the Professor Aurelius Augustine. There is no doubt at all that it was this extraordinary episode which more than anything else hastened the conversion of St. Augustine. He never forgot those Catholic hymns then heard for the first time, as their sound floated across the ring of soldiery from the besieged basilica to where he stood in the moonlight, wrapped in his cloak, anxious for his dear old mother Monica imprisoned in the church.

And now the calm endurance of Ambrose had won the day, and the Arian attack was defeated. The Bishop determined that the approaching consecration of the basilica which is now called St. Ambrogio should be a solemn thanksgiving for the victory of the Faith. And a great and wonderful sign of divine blessing attended it.

The search for the relics of the martyrs Gervasius and Protasius, who had died in the persecution under Nero, was successful. St. Ambrose had earnestly desired that they should lie beneath the altar of the new church, and the brothers were found, as tradition had suggested that they would be, locked in each other's arms, for they had been killed by one blow. They were carried in rapturous triumph to the spot where some of you have venerated St. Ambrose, who now lies between them, in the basilica which thus commemorates the triumph of the Faith.

Miracles attended the procession of the relics, and miracles, the evidence for which is first-rate. St Ambrose and St. Augustine both describe these miracles themselves, and indeed they are as well attested as any in history. The fact is that miracles need a certain atmosphere of faith and anticipation. Our Lord Himself could do no mighty works in certain places because of the atmosphere of unbelief. But the triumph of the Catholic religion under the faithful Ambrose created such an atmosphere, and so our Lord passed through the streets of Milan by the bier of the holy martyrs, and blind men received their sight, the lame walked, the lepers were cleansed, and the deaf heard.

That shrine in the Church of St. Ambrogio is holy ground indeed.

V

THE scenes which we saw at the end of the last chapter were scenes of contest and triumph. We watched the siege of the Catholics in the great basilica during the Arian struggles inspired by the Empress Justina, the victory of Ambrose and its celebration, the consecration of the church now dedicated to him, and the miracles which attended it.

In the following year there occurred a miracle far more important than any of them, the conversion of the Professor Aurelius Augustinus, who became that great doctor of the Church—St. Augustine of Hippo. All our conceptions of Christianity come to us filtered through the mind of St. Augustine. To us Westerns St. Augustine is, after St. Peter and St. Paul, the most important saint in the calendar. The constancy of the Catholics in the Arian troubles had made a profound impression on Augustine's mind. St. Monica, his mother, had been shut up in the besieged basilica " living on prayer," St. Augustine says, and it was to the spiritual efforts of these times that under God we must attribute his conversion.

And now once more the fortunes of St. Ambrose are linked with those of the Empire. You remember that an arrangement had been come to with the usurper Maximus by which he was to retain France, Spain and Great Britain on the understanding that he did not make any attempts on Italy and the Danube provinces. Since then, Maximus had sought to strengthen his position by a profession of Catholic orthodoxy. There was practically no Arianism in his part of the Empire, and his profession of piety was applauded by the bishops and laity over whom he ruled. For some time he had been growing discontented with the treaty which had fixed his frontiers, and now the Arian disturbances at Milan gave him an opportunity for interfering in the dominions of Valentinian. He wrote a letter of protest against the recent treatment of Catholics to the young Emperor, but the object of the letter lay in the postscript. Maximus started a grievance. He said that Valentinian was not respecting his frontiers, and further, that his employment of the German tribes as recruiting centres strengthened them for aggressive action against Gaul.

Ambrose had been the diplomatist who had arranged

the delimitation of frontiers, and he had to be summoned to the palace to discuss the position. A less noble man might have been tempted into disloyalty by Maximus' profession of orthodoxy, but Ambrose was not moved. Notwithstanding the cruelties into which the heresy of Justina had led the boy Emperor, Ambrose remained unswervingly loyal, and so we have the extraordinary situation of the ecclesiastical rebel of the day before being sent again as Imperial ambassador to Maximus at Treves. It was important that Maximus should not see that Valentinian had read between the lines of the threatening letter. It was necessary, therefore, to invent a pretext for sending so distinguished a person as Ambrose, and they made the body of Gratian the pretext. Gratian's body still lay in Gaul. Ambrose was to go to Treves to negotiate for its removal; incidentally he was to deal with the other matters.

If you would keep a clear picture of the Bishop in your mind during all these events, you must remember that all the while he is the ascetic and man of prayer, and that the Liturgy, his office, his studies, the government of the Church, the care of the poor and afflicted, all the while have the first place in his mind.

The letter of Maximus had been a threat. Ambrose arrives at Treves a tremendous figure, who meets the threat with a counter-offensive. His spirit was really superb. He found Treves racked with a religious controversy of the most acute type, and his first concern is to define his attitude towards it. Maximus, the Catholic *poseur*, and his sycophantic Gallican bishops had gone over the border line between strictness and cruelty, and had put to death the heretic Priscillian and some of his followers. The greatest of all the bishops of Gaul had made his protest—St. Martin of Tours had refused to communicate with the bishops who had applauded the execution of Priscillian, and had withdrawn from the Court of Maximus.

Who was Priscillian ? And what were the Priscillianists ? Priscillian had latterly been Bishop of Avila in Spain, long afterwards the birthplace of St. Theresa, and Priscillian was a Mrs. Besant who had a following as fanatical as the following of Mrs. Mary Baker Eddy. His religion was a mixture of astrology, theosophy and Christianity, and it raged for a time with great violence. There is no doubt that the Bishops of Gaul were thoroughly frightened by it, and they concurred in the persecution and execution of the leading people. St. Ambrose was horrified when he learnt that Catholics had shed blood in the defence of the Faith, and he declined communion with the Bishops of Gaul, and therefore also with the Emperor.

Observe the extraordinary position he was in. The greatest champion of Catholicism comes to Treves as the Ambassador of an Arian Emperor, and when he gets there he renounces communion with the Catholic Bishops and Emperor owing to the cruel excesses they had committed in defence of the Faith. The Holy Spirit alone can guide a man through such a tangle as that.

I must dwell at some length on this mission to Treves, because it shows us the Bishop in a strong light. After Maximus had agreed to accept the Western portion of the Empire he had come to regard himself as the *de jure* possessor of the whole and Valentinian II as his vassal. When he heard that Ambrose was coming he determined to receive him in a manner which would suggest this. An ambassador of a friendly power would be received in private audience. Maximus ordered that Ambrose should be received as a suppliant at the Public Consistory—a court for hearing causes of all sorts presided over by the Emperor. I always wonder whether Ambrose enjoyed the joke of what followed or whether in those days one would do in dead seriousness what to-day one could not do without an interior smile.

Imagine the grand hall crowded with officials, at the upper end the dais, the throne, and the Emperor on the throne. Ambrose is announced, and he enters the hall through the great doors at the further end. Maximus rises and advances three steps, and then stands on the dais waiting to bestow the kiss of peace on Ambrose. Ambrose also takes three paces up the hall and then stands immovable.

Officials glide up to him. "Your lordship must proceed up the hall and ascend the dais, where his Clemency will receive you."

Ambrose remains immovable.

"Your lordship is keeping his Clemency waiting. I must beg you to advance."

Ambrose remains immovable.

Then the Emperor : "Bishop, I am waiting to give you the kiss of peace."

Then Ambrose, from the other end of the enormous hall : "Why do you want to kiss a man whose name you do not know ? If you knew who I am you would not receive me here."

Maximus goes back to his throne and sits down. "You are angry, Bishop."

"And not without reason. I am amazed at being received here."

"But the last time you came you were received in Consistory."

"The last time I came, I came to sue for peace; to-day I come as the ambassador of an equal."

"An equal! An equal! To whom does Valentinian owe it that he is equal to me?"

"He owes it to God Almighty, for God has preserved for him the power He gave him."

The Emperor jumps up. "Yes, you tricked me, you and that Bauto who is reigning in the boy's name and strengthening the barbarians against me. If I had not stopped of my own accord when you came, what was there to balk me?"

"Do not lose your temper, your Clemency. There is not the slightest need for it. Listen calmly to what I am going to say."

Then Ambrose made his speech and dealt with all the matters he had come to deal with. It was an exceedingly caustic speech, and Maximus cut him short after a time, and told him in a floundering sort of way that he would consider the matter under discussion.

Next day he ordered Ambrose out of Treves, and everybody told Ambrose that he must go by night and by a circuitous route, as it was known that ambuscades would be set in his path and that he would be murdered. Ambrose left in broad daylight and took the usual route. He took with him a poor old Gallican Bishop who had repented of consenting to the execution of the Priscillianists. He sent a swift courier before him with a minute account of what had happened. The authorities were greatly perturbed. Ambrose had failed, they said, by his lack of persuasiveness, and they sent another ambassador, Domninus, with instructions that he must be very suave and conciliatory. He was— and so was Maximus. So kind was Maximus that he even offered to send a force into Italy to help his brother Valentinian against the tribes of Pannonia. Domninus himself was to command the force. Maximus must have been very clever, for Domninus led the army Maximus had given him through the Alps, past all the fortresses and garrisons. Maximus followed hard behind with all the other troops he could muster. He overtook Domninus twenty miles from Milan, took over the command of the whole, and appeared as invader before the gates of the city. The Court fled to Aquileia, and soon after Justina and Valentinian went off to Salonica and placed themselves under the protection of the Eastern Emperor, the great Theodosius. Only one man of note remained in Milan. That man was the Bishop St. Ambrose.

Theodosius had lately completed the restoration of order in the East. Theodosius was a Lord Kitchener: he was the big, strong, silent, patient, diligent soldier. He always knew that some day he must deal with Maximus, and now he felt the time had come. He received Valentinian very kindly ; he took the boy into his arms and kissed him tenderly. " My boy," he said, " let this misfortune teach you a lesson. The man who drove you out of Milan offers a more adequate worship to Christ than you do; his strength therefore lies in your unfaithfulness."

Valentinian was a charming boy of fifteen; he flung his arms around Theodosius and he said, "I will never again forsake the law of Christ."

"And so," said Ambrose afterwards, "it is not the Empire your Clemency gave back to young Valentinian, it is himself that you have given back to the Faith."

Meanwhile affairs were not going well with the usurping Maximus in Italy. Ambrose would have nothing to do with him, and the Catholics in general gave him the cold shoulder. He tried to curry favour with the Pagans by proclaiming the equality of all religions, and there was a slight, spasmodic effort to repair Pagan shrines and restore Pagan cults, but there was no enthusiasm. Theodosius had married Galla, the daughter of Justina, and his armies were gathering in the East. He met Maximus in two months and completely routed him. The soldiers went over to the stronger man; they stripped the wretched Maximus of his purple and dragged him to Theodosius' tent. Maximus was executed. Theodosius restored Valentinian to his throne in Milan.

A new interest now enters into the story of Ambrose, the relation between these tremendously strong men, Ambrose and Theodosius—who was virtually Emperor of the West as well as the East. Hitherto Ambrose had guided and rebuked boy Emperors. How would the great Bishop fare with one of the strongest men of any age? He was no longer called upon to take a share in affairs of state; Theodosius was capable of doing all his business for himself. Ambrose felt this to be a

great relief. For the rest of his life he is the great
Catholic prelate, and that alone ; but where Catholic
interests were at stake there at once Ambrose was in
the field, sword in hand. The first reason for inter-
vention arose over an attempted resuscitation of our old
friend the goddess of victory.

The Roman Senate sent a deputation to Milan to beg
Theodosius to visit Rome. His great conquests, it
suggested, formed a fitting opportunity to restore to
Rome the traditional rites and ceremonies of victory.
Theodosius gave them no answer to this part of the
request. St. Ambrose was alarmed. He went to
the palace and spoke plainly. Theodosius, annoyed at
being spoken to with such frankness, did not feel he
could yield at once to dictation, so Ambrose absented
himself for a time from the court. This had the desired
effect. Theodosius thought out the whole matter
and determined on a policy of uncompromising Catholicism. His visit to Rome, which was very brilliant,
produced a mass of conversions to the Faith, the value
of which I should reckon rather more than doubtful.

Meanwhile the Emperor was greatly annoyed by
reports from the East of Catholic and Arian riots ; both
sides behaved deplorably, and Theodosius was prepared
to mete out equal punishment all round, but his son
Arcadius, whom he had raised to Imperial rank and had
left to represent him in the East, told his father that
his position would be intolerable if he had to begin
his life of office by punishing all classes of his subjects.
He said the Arians were repentant, and Theodosius
forgave them. He was more angry, and rightly more
angry, with the Catholics and he was less disposed to be

lenient to them. This brought him into instant collision with St. Ambrose, over a particular case. It was said that the Bishop of Callinicum had incited his monks to acts of violence and to the destruction of heretical buildings. The case was not investigated with sufficient care, and the Bishop was hastily ordered to rebuild at his own cost all the buildings which had been destroyed, including a Jewish synagogue.

St. Ambrose was away at the time, but when he heard that a bishop had been ordered to rebuild a synagogue he wrote an uncompromising protest. He laid it down in this letter, as an absolute rule of the Church, that no bishop could raise a building in which the Faith would be misrepresented, or traduced, without sacrilege.

At the end of the letter he hinted in veiled terms that if the Emperor persisted in this order he would excommunicate him. Of this letter the Emperor took no notice.

The thing had happened far away, and most of the people who saw the scene which ensued in the basilica did not know what it meant.

On the first Sunday on which Theodosius appeared at the Solemn Eucharist in the basilica, after Ambrose's return, Ambrose had a sermon ready for him; he preached from the text, " I see a rod," and the rod he referred to was Apostolic authority—as an illustration of this he quotes Nathan's rebuke to David. Theodosius began to look uncomfortable, and Ambrose noticing this, stopped dead, and said : " Yes, Emperor, yes, I speak not only of you but to you."

When he came down from the pulpit it would be natural for him to go at once to the altar and begin the liturgy, but Theodosius rose and walked to meet him.

"It was me, then, that you were preaching against?"

"Yes. I thought it would be useful to you."

"I admit it was hard to make the bishop rebuild the synagogue, and I have rescinded the order, but monks do a great deal of harm."

Here the Master of the Horse interpolated some very improper remarks upon the religious life.

"I am not speaking to you," said Ambrose, "I am speaking to the Emperor who has the fear of the Lord in him. If I addressed you who have used such indecent language, I should speak in another key. Now, your Clemency, let me go to the altar with a good heart. Take this burden off my soul."

The Emperor sat down again. "Very good," he said, "now go on with the liturgy."

Ambrose remained immovable. "You must cancel the order altogether," he said.

"I will do so," said the Emperor.

"I go then to the altar, on your solemn word, on your solemn word," said Ambrose.

"Go to the altar on my solemn word," said Theodosius.

And so the episode of the synagogue at Callinicum was closed.

Perhaps we do not altogether sympathize with Ambrose here, but he has given us reason to trust him and I have no doubt that at that moment the refusal to rebuild the synagogue was necessary, although we may not feel the underlying principle to be operative for all time.

And now we reach the great tragedy of our tale.

Thessalonica was a great Catholic city devoted to Theodosius. It celebrated his victories by brilliant rejoicings.
There was a great charioteer in Thessalonica who was
the idol of the patrons of the circus. This man was a
very bad man, and the governor imprisoned him just
at this time for disgraceful offences. The whole city
rose in revolt, the mob overmastered the army, they
killed the governor and his staff, they butchered the
soldiers, they tore their dead bodies limb from limb
and paraded the city waving the fragments in the air.

Theodosius was a very self-controlled man, but when
he heard this news he had a sort of brain storm. He
really went mad for the moment. " The whole town
shall suffer for this," he said, " for the whole town is
guilty." He left Milan for fear Ambrose should balk
him of his vengeance, and after a while he struck. The
people were collected into the immense theatre and the
soldiers were given leave to attack them as they pleased
to avenge their comrades.

The soldiers were mad for revenge, and the massacre
which ensued extended from one end of the town to
the other.

There is no doubt that when Theodosius awoke from
his delirium of anger he was horror-struck and conscience-
stricken at once, but the deed was done.

From end to end of the Empire public feeling was
outraged, and every eye was turned on the Bishop of
Milan.

What would Ambrose do ? He was ill at the time,
and he did nothing hastily. After his convalescence
in the country when he came back to Milan he did not
go, as was his custom, to present his duty to the Emperor.

He was silent. After a few days he wrote. " I have left you alone until now," he said, " that your natural piety might exhibit itself freely in contrition. Now I must act. You must do public penance before the Empire. Until you have done that I cannot offer the Holy Sacrifice in your presence again." Ambrose made no proposals as to the details of the penance. He left all that to Theodosius. Theodosius made no move, and the Sunday came on which, according to custom, the Emperor and court would go to the basilica for Mass.

We can see the scene. We know the atrium of St. Ambrogio, which preserves the features of it—if it is not the very spot. In the doorway facing the court stood the Bishop in his pontificals, a solitary figure in the strong sunlight against the gloom of the interior. He barred the Emperor's path.

" Stop, Emperor, you do not understand the gravity of the crime you have committed. Your great power blinds you. Your reason is darkened by your being free to do what you please. For us all there is indeed but one Emperor, He who is the Creator of all things. With what eyes will you look now upon the Temple of our Lord ? With what feet will you dare to tread His Sanctuary ? How will you dare to lift up to Him your blood-stained hands ? How can such hands touch the Sacred Body of Christ ? How will you lift His Blood to those lips by whose angry words has been shed the blood of so many of the innocent ? Retire, lest entering here you add to yourself yet another sin. Accept the bond the Sovereign Lord imposes on you—a remedy which will bring back health to your soul."

The head of Theodosius sank on his breast. Slowly he turned, and with his court went back into the streets of the city.

But he made no movement. For eight months all relations between the Church and the palace were suspended. Then Christmas came. Would the Emperor be restored at Christmas?

The Prefect, the Lord Chamberlain, found him one day sitting solitary, his face wet with tears.

"What is the matter?" said the Chamberlain, cheerily.

"You laugh, Rufinus," said Theodosius, "but you do not know how I suffer. The beggars and thieves go to church, but its gates and the gates of heaven are closed to me."

"I will go off to the Bishop," said Rufinus. "I will get this put straight."

"He will never relent," said the Emperor.

"Nevertheless, I will go," said Rufinus.

"And I will follow you immediately," said the Emperor.

When Ambrose heard Rufinus had come just before the liturgy he thought the Emperor meant to force his way in. "What brings you here?" he cried. "What is your shameless purpose? You counselled the massacre."

"The Emperor is coming," said Rufinus. "I beg you not to refuse him."

"If he attempts to cross the threshold of the church," said Ambrose, "I will repel him with my own hands. And if he chooses to murder me I will give my body to his sword."

Rufinus ran back and met the Emperor and his staff, who were now half-way to the church. "Do not attempt it, your Clemency," he said.

"I am going on," said the Emperor. "I am going to submit to the humiliation I deserve."

Once again Ambrose stood on the threshold of the church.

"I beg you to release me from my sin," said Theodosius.

"What do you want?" said Ambrose. "What daring brings you here?"

"I am not come to dare," said Theodosius, "but to ask for deliverance. I beg you, in the name of mercy and of our Lord, not to shut the door on me, which is open to every sinner that repents." The door was open, but there was a great bar put across the opening.

"What are the signs of your repentance?"

"It is for you to point out to me what I must do," said Theodosius.

Ink, parchment and a table were brought.

"Your Majesty must pass and sign a decree to the effect that no confiscation or death may take effect until thirty days after sentence, and that in that time the sentence is to be reviewed, and if necessary revised."

The Emperor wrote and signed the decree.

Then Ambrose stood aside, the bar was drawn back, and Theodosius entered. As he crossed the threshold he flung himself on his face on the floor and kissed the pavement.

"My soul cleaveth to the dust," he cried. "O quicken Thou me according to Thy word."

Ambrose sang Mass, but the Blessed Sacrament was not brought to the throne as usual for the Emperor's communion. A messenger came from the altar. " The Bishop says, Your Majesty, that you will come to the altar to-day in the crowd."

So Theodosius came back among the humble and poor to the altar of the Lord. " Only Ambrose," he used to say years after, " ever showed me what a Bishop is."

VI

IT was in December, 390, that Theodosius did penance. St. Ambrose died in April, 397. I must now give some account of the last seven years of his life.

It is a story of disappointed hopes. Ambrose had had a wonderful vision of a Holy Roman Empire, of a perfect correlation of the Church and State, but when he died the Empire was hastening to its fall : Alaric, the Goth, was rising into view, and far behind him on the eastern horizon there already dawned the awful menace of the Huns.

I have been asked why it was that after the massacre of Thessalonica, the whole Empire looked for action from the Bishop of Milan. The answer is that Milan had been the working capital of the West for some time, and that Theodosius lived there for the greater part of three years after the conquest of Maximus and the restoration to his throne of the young Valentinian II. This was why the onus of dealing with the matter lay with St. Ambrose, although I am bound to say that I think he would have seen that it was dealt with in whatever part of the Empire Theodosius might have been living. You observe that during these three years the great Eastern Emperor was living in the West, and the young Western Emperor was content to act under his tutelage. But such a state of affairs could not go on. Theodosius was urgently needed in the East; he returned there in the spring of 392.

The penance of Theodosius had produced upon him the effect we should expect—it had greatly strengthened his religion; he was now a more militant champion of Catholicism than ever. Young Valentinian followed his example; he had flung aside the rags of his Arianism, and he grew into a feeling of attachment to Ambrose as devoted as that of his brother Gratian. His life was a model of piety, austerity and prayer, and he set his hand to a task to which he at length fell a martyr, to the task of reforming the Imperial court. You can imagine how paganism would linger in a thousand forms in a court, owing to the innate conservatism of the institution. These gentle and chaste Imperial boys of the earliest days of the conquest of Christianity are extraordinarily pathetic figures. Valentinian II lived with his two sisters, the Princesses Justa and Grata, who, under St. Ambrose's direction, were leading lives of the deepest devotion and persevering towards perfection.

There was a bitter party against the beautiful young trio, but when Valentinian II was told of palace plots he only smiled. He might have won his way in the end and sent the hateful old palace system, with its favourites, intrigues and venality, to limbo had not Theodosius made the fatal mistake of appointing the

general Arbogastes, who was a Goth by descent, to be
the military tutor and adviser of Valentinian. Arbogastes was a brilliant soldier and Theodosius felt he had
every reason to trust him; but face to face with the
Catholic party of the palace, and its inspirer St. Ambrose,
the innate paganism of Arbogastes awoke. He was of
Lord Melbourne's opinion that the Church has nothing
to do with a man's private life. There was a quiet
strength in the young Emperor which opposed itself
to Arbogastes on points of principle from time to time,
and Arbogastes rightly attributed this to this Catholic
piety.

And so the long struggle between the two began.
Gradually Arbogastes surrounded the Emperor with
servants who were really his jailers; then he brought
influence to bear upon him to move his court into Gaul
under the pretext that the Western portion of the Empire
would be the better for the occasional presence of the
Emperor. When he got him there he alienated all the
local magnates from him. Valentinian sent letters of
distress to Theodosius, but it took long to get letters
to Constantinople and they were easily intercepted on
the way.

Once more the Roman senators came demanding the
restoration of the altar of victory. Once more a Catholic
Emperor refused them. Then at last came the scene
on which the story turns.

One day Arbogastes entered the consistory of the
Emperor with a military order which needed the Imperial
signature. Valentinian laid it aside and handed Arbogastes another paper. It contained his dismissal from
all his posts.

Arbogastes tore it into a hundred pieces and flung them on the pavement, saying: " You did not make me what I am and cannot unmake me."

Then the unhappy boy Emperor lost his self-control; he sprang at Arbogastes and pulled his sword out of its scabbard.

" Would you kill me ? " cried Arbogastes.

" No, myself," said the Emperor. " I would rather die than reign without the power of ruling."

Officials sprang between the two men, and the consistory broke up in confusion.

After this Valentinian tried to get Ambrose to come to him, and failed. The letters were so reticent that Ambrose failed to read between the lines. He did not think it advisable to go into Gaul to deal with things of State. Valentinian had not yet been baptized. He was trying to get back to Italy, where he would be safer ; as his pretext, he said he wished to go in person against the mountain tribes who were threatening Illyria, and he begged Ambrose to come to Gaul to baptize him before he set out. Ambrose knew that his coming to do this would give the greatest offence to the bishops of Gaul. It needed a great deal to persuade him that his presence in Gaul was desirable. At last he fixed a day for his departure. Then it was announced, untruly, that the Emperor was coming to Milan; that caused a further delay, and when at last he set out it was too late.

Day after day the Emperor waited for messages from Ambrose: every night before he went to bed, every morning when he awoke he asked the question, " Has my messenger returned from the Bishop of Milan ? "

The certainty that the Bishop was coming, and that he would carry all before him, sealed the Emperor's fate.

The scene in the consistory furnished the tale which was circulated about his death; it was announced that in a fit of passion he had committed suicide—as a matter of fact he was assassinated, and is said to have died crying to Ambrose for help.

Arbogastes professed great distress at the Emperor's supposed suicide, and he sent his body with great pomp to Italy. On the Italian side of the Alps, the Bishop of Milan and his attendants, travelling to Gaul, met the funeral cortege of Valentinian on its way to Milan. The shock to Ambrose was appalling. "If you had gone before," said the people, "this might not have happened."

Ambrose's reasons for delay had been good ones, but he, too, felt this with bitter grief.

He brought the young Emperor's body back with tears, and amid the tears of all the people. He wrote to Theodosius for directions about the obsequies. Meanwhile the Princesses Justa and Grata and the sorrowing people kept vigil round the body of the dead boy.

St. Ambrose's letter to Theodosius was a very delicate piece of diplomacy; it was to remind him that a tremendous crisis was at hand; it was to make a direct link with Theodosius over the matter without in any way stepping outside his own province.

The crisis developed. Arbogastes could not seize the throne, his Gothic descent and name alone made that impossible at the moment, so he got the army to proclaim a clever journalist, called Eugenius, Emperor, while he and the army kept the actual power in their own hands.

A deputation, consisting of a pagan advocate and some sycophantic bishops, started for Constantinople to inform Theodosius as to what had happened and to ask his recognition of the Emperor Eugenius. Meanwhile the reply of Theodosius to Ambrose arrived and the State funeral of Valentinian was held.

The oration of Ambrose over the dead body of Valentinian lasted an hour, and it had all the subtlety and skill of Mark Antony's oration over the body of Cæsar. Ambrose cannot accuse Arbogastes openly, so he attacks Maximus for the murder of Gratian: everyone in the basilica reading Arbogastes and Valentinian for Maximus and Gratian. You can gather the style from the opening words: " Valentinian has come, but not as we expected. He did not fail in his promise to us. He heard that the Alps, the defence of Italy, were threatened by a barbarian foe, and he chose danger to share our dangers. This, then, has been the Emperor's crime, that he would have saved the Roman Empire ! Who so distorted a noble plan as to make it a crime ? Who ? "

Then a little later : " He dies while yet he treads the very entrance of the path of life. I speak of the suddenness of his death, not of its mode; my voice is not the voice of the accuser, it is the voice of the mourner."

When they left the basilica that day it was clear to the crowd that there could be no peace between Ambrose and the Emperor Eugenius, yet Ambrose had not said a word which his enemies could lay hold of. Eugenius sent him a formal notice of his accession. Ambrose took no notice of it. There is no doubt that next to Theodosius, Ambrose was the figure which most often disturbed the new Emperor's dreams. Arbogastes and he had begun their joint careers by a successful campaign against the tribes of the Rhine, and even at the peace banquet, far away from Milan, the ghost of Ambrose rose.

One of the barbarian chiefs suddenly said to Arbogastes, " Do you know the man they call Ambrose ? "

" Yes," said Arbogastes, considerably startled. " Yes, I dine with him sometimes."

" Ah," said the chief, " that accounts for your successes; you are the friend of a man who says to the sun, ' Stop ! ' and it stops."

Eugenius was a Christian in name, but in reality only a devotee of the arts, and the pagan party had hopes of him. They made their usual request that the altar of victory might be restored. This was refused, but a second application for a relaxation of the laws against pagan observances was more successful. Some of the temple revenues were to be given to the pagan party, whose members were called " those of the Gentile observance"—a delightful euphemism which I commend to some of our controversialists to-day—and pagan rites and ceremonies were no longer to be penal.

These concessions of Eugenius gave Ambrose an excuse for declining all communication with him. When this *parvenu* Emperor arrived in Milan the Bishop was not there. Ambrose had gone away and left Milan to choose between Eugenius and himself. The people received the Emperor with aversion and in silence, and the clergy refused his gifts in the basilica. Mean-

146

while the progress of St. Ambrose through the cities
of Italy was one long triumph. He comforted the
penitent, strengthened the religious, healed the sick,
and in the case of the boy Pansophius, at Florence—
whom he dealt with after the manner of the prophet
Elisha—he is even said to have raised the dead.

While Eugenius pandered to paganism at Milan,
and Ambrose revived the scenes of apostolic days in the
cities of Italy, Theodosius was arming himself in the
East for a holy war : he was preparing to destroy this
resuscitated paganism and the wretched creature Eugenius, who had permitted it.

When he realized this, Arbogastes decided to come
out as the undisguised champion of paganism. So
Hercules was set once more on his pedestal, the auspices
and the entrails of the victims were consulted, pagan
standards were restored to the Western army, and
Arbogastes left for the front shaking his fist at the
Christians. "We will come back the conquerors,"
he cried, "and turn their churches into stables and their
priests into soldiers."

As Eugenius and Arbogastes left Milan the Bishop,
St. Ambrose, re-entered it, undaunted by these threats.
The battle was fought on the Isonzo—where Italians
and Austrians fought in the late war. The first engage-
ment seemed to show that Arbogastes had the superiority,
and the generals of Theodosius counselled a retreat until
reinforcements could come up, but Theodosius replied :
"The cross shall never fall back for a day before an
idol." A little chapel stood perched on the hill on which
the Catholic army was drawn up. Theodosius went
into the chapel at nightfall, and prostrating himself

upon the ground, he spent the night in prayer; in the early morning he had a vision of St. John and St. Philip, who promised him their aid. It was the 7th September, and at dawn a great wind arose and blew clouds of dust in the eyes of the pagans. Eugenius, sword in hand, advanced through the storm, shouting, " Where is the Lord God of Theodosius ? " Once more some of the enemy forces went over to his side, and the confusion was so great that Eugenius thought that messengers had come to tell him of the capture of Theodosius, when in reality they had come to capture him. He was beheaded with a single stroke, the while kneeling at Theodosius' feet. At Milan St. Ambrose laid the letter which announced the victory on the altar of the basilica and went with great thankfulness to meet Theodosius at Aquileia. He went partly to see that Theodosius was merciful to his enemies, and he secured their pardon. At last, he thought, the day of the Christian Empire has dawned, but he was wrong. Four months afterwards Theodosius lay dead in front of the altar of the basilica of Milan, and the Bishop preached his funeral sermon before a timid little boy of twelve, who sat weeping bitterly on the Imperial throne. By the side of little Honorius stood his strong, rough, Gothic tutor, Stilicho, whom prosperity was to corrupt into an unscrupulous politician, who strengthened and enriched himself while he gave his time and talents to the Empire. Somewhere in the congregation that day stood a young Gothic officer, who was on the eve of departing with his regiment for Germany; his companions named him the Bold. He stood there silent and unobserved, and saw the last heroic Emperor pass to his tomb. Next year he began the hostilities which fifteen years later laid Rome in ruins, for his name was Alaric.

St. Ambrose survived Theodosius only two years. In some respects they were years of sadness and disappointment. Venal officials surrounded a baby Emperor, and any contact with the court must have been displeasing to the Bishop. On the other hand, the Faith was in a stronger position than ever before, and there were strong men ready to sustain the burden of affairs when Ambrose laid it down.

In the west, Augustine was growing into the maturity of Christian strength, and in the east John Chrysostom was drawing near to his tenure of the patriarchal throne of Constantinople.

St. Ambrose had one more great battle with the Western authorities before he died: it was over the privilege of sanctuary. A condemned criminal had managed to escape and had taken refuge at the altar of a church; the State officials broke sanctuary and reclaimed him. Ambrose was entirely right in fighting this. Sanctuary made a very rough and ready court of ecclesiastical appeal from civil injustice; there was no injustice in this particular case, but it was exceedingly important to preserve the right for the disorderly times that were coming. It helped also to impress on the popular imagination the majesty of the Church's claim to be the refuge of her children in their extremity.

There was a great popular clamour against the authorities and Ambrose won the day once more. Stilicho modified the man's sentence and he was not executed.

But in Ambrose the sword had at last worn out the scabbard, and the Bishop longed for death. He went through the discipline of mental despondency. The world of Stilicho and Honorius was a new world and a disordered failing one. Ambrose's dream had proved to be empty. Our Lord was now showing his great servant that he would never reign from the Palatine. An irresistible sadness overwhelmed Ambrose. " I am no use to anyone," he said. " I long to be at rest and have the joy of committing no more sin."

One of his latest treatises is entitled *De bono mortis*, on the benefit of death.

" O my Father," he prays, " open Thine arms to receive the poor servant who cries to Thee. Open wide Thy bosom to receive me, and with me all those who have believed in the Lord. They are many, for the Faith has grown exceedingly, but iniquity abounds and the love of many has grown cold."

He was working at this time at his commentary on the 43rd Psalm. He was not well enough to write himself, and his young secretary was writing at his dictation. When he reached the 23rd verse—" Up, Lord, why sleepest Thou ? Awake, and be not absent from us for ever "—he broke off and said in a dreamy, wistful tone, " It is hard indeed to wait so long for the day which is to swallow up the shadow of death. Rise, Lord, why sleepest Thou ? How long wilt Thou cast me off ? "

There was a pause, the secretary looked up and he saw the face of the saint transfigured. It seemed as though flames played about his forehead and about his lips, and his face became white like snow.

The fingers of the secretary grew stiff with a spasm of holy fear; he laid his pen down; no word was spoken,

but it was tacitly understood that Ambrose would work
no more, and that is why his commentary on the 43rd
Psalm ends with that verse.

Towards the end of February, 397, Ambrose took
to his bed and his illness became critical.

Stilicho, the rough and brutal ruler of the country,
who seems to me to have been very much like one of
those unscrupulous American millionaires who make
corners in wheat and build churches and schools, was
genuinely distressed and even alarmed.

" The day that great man dies," he said, " will be
the destruction of Italy."

He did a very odd thing—he sent a big deputation
of notables to the dying Bishop to beg the Bishop not
to die. Ambrose must have smiled. " I am not
ashamed to live," he said, " and I am not afraid to die.
We have a good Master."

Milan was most deeply moved, and prayer was
offered unceasingly. The clergy surrounded him day
and night. Who in the world would succeed Ambrose ?
It is not surprising that those who watched in the big
chamber where the Bishop lay should debate the question
in undertones. One day four of them were talking of
this, well out of earshot, as they thought, of the dying
man, and named Simplicianus, when they were startled
by a strong, musing voice from the bed, " Old, but good,"
said Ambrose musingly, " old but good, old but good."
Simplicianus was his successor.

He lingered until Good Friday, which that year fell
on April 3rd. When he felt his agony to be begun,
Ambrose stretched out his arms in the form of the crucifix.
He only moved his arms once, but his lips kept moving

all the time. After midnight Honoratus, Bishop of Vercelli, who had been watching, went to his room to take some rest. As he lay down a voice said to him, " Rise again, hasten, he is going. Rise again, hasten, he is going. Rise again, hasten, he is going." Honoratus went to the church and brought the Blessed Sacrament at once. When Ambrose saw the Blessed Sacrament he drew his outstretched arms together in the gesture of prayer. He received Viaticum, then he stretched out his arms again and died.

On Easter morning they carried him into the church which bears his name. All the Christians surrounded him, and with them were the Jews, and the Pagans too; all men did homage to him that day as he lay in peace in the Ambrosian basilica.

His body lies there still, and his spirit reigns with Christ.

ATHANASIUS CONTRA MUNDUM

ALEXANDRIA was a wonderful city at the beginning of the fourth century. It was long but not broad, like Brighton, with the sea in front and a lake behind, canals joining the two. It had enormous and magnificent water-frontages on three sides, with great granite quays at which ships could anchor. I do not think those great cities of long ago were interesting; they must have been very like the Shepherd's Bush " White City " built of real marble. But Alexandria was in three sections: the old Egyptian quarter with its great temple of Serapis, which had all the Egyptian weirdness of form and brilliancy of colour; the great Jewish quarter; and the modern imperial city, with the world-famous library joined to the other public buildings by immense marble colonnades, which were decorated with busts and with sphinxes and figures looted from the fallen temples of Upper Egypt.

The fourth century was not a young age like the twelfth in Italy and the sixteenth in England. It was a declining age like the period in which we live. Then, as now, men were disillusioned, imitative, æsthetic, antiquarian. Then, as now, public opinion was inclined to pick out of all systems, Jewish, Pagan, Christian, what it considered worth keeping of each. The old hatred of Christianity had disappeared, it was a mark of superiority to be tolerant of all religions.

Such was the moment at which the Church fought and won the battle of her essential assertion—Jesus Christ is Final—Jesus Christ is God, there is no other further force in the Universe behind Him. In Him you behold all there is. She fought it not against frank adversaries, but against false brethren who claimed to believe all that she believed, with one slight shade of a qualifying difference about the finality of Jesus Christ. The difference on paper was actually the difference of one letter, *iota*, the smallest letter of the Greek alphabet. But the difference, though microscopic to look at, was really infinite, and over that *iota* Athanasius endured his most bitter passion.

Athanasius was the most fascinating person imaginable. He was very delicately beautiful—like Dr. Liddon as a young man—and he had the magnetic charm of John Henry Newman. He had all Newman's natural sensitiveness, and all the acquired sensitiveness of an age like our own. At one moment he had to face martyrdom, and he dreaded it just as Newman would have dreaded it. There was nothing Chinese about Athanasius. But he had perfect moral courage, and people found the combination of sensitiveness, faithfulness, tenderness and courage quite irresistible. When he returned to Alexandria after his exiles the people used to carpet the streets and illuminate the city.

Like Liddon, he was recognized in his boyhood as the heaven-born ecclesiastic. It was always clear that as soon as he was old enough he must be given high office in the Church, and he became Archdeacon of Alexandria and secretary to the Archbishop Alexander while still a youthful prodigy.

In those days the Alexandrian Papacy was only second to the Roman. Athanasius began his career as Cardinal-secretary to the Egyptian Pope, and as such he found himself behind the scenes at the Council of Nicæa, which had been summoned by the newly-converted Emperor Constantine to decide the term in which the Church should define the Deity of our Lord.

Nicæa, twenty miles from Nicomedia, was a sort of official suburb of the seat of government, a sort of Potsdam, a modern rectilinear town full of smart imperial officials. Hither came 318 Bishops; and when they were gathered together in a great hall of the palace, they presented so moving a sight that Constantine wept as he stood among them. Many of them had come from the asceticism of the deserts, and many others were branded, broken and mutilated by the awful persecutions which Athanasius, young as he was, remembered. But no single Bishop counted heavily at Nicæa. There were really two antagonists: one was the rector of an important Alexandrian church, Arius; the other was the young Archdeacon Athanasius.

Arius was attractive too, a loose-limbed giant, handsome, pale, thin, ascetic, with downcast face and a fierce, eager way of speaking. He fascinated men, and still more women, as he stood before them swinging his arms violently and pouring out torrents of argument on behalf of what he insisted was Bible Christianity.

The point before the Council was a simple one: Is the Son co-equal with the Father? If not, He is a creature after all, and God could conceivably produce another such. Which does the Church believe? And the Arians were saying, " For pity's sake don't let that

question be answered; let us all agree to accept the Bible
and leave it at that, and then we can't go wrong."

It was the same latitudinarian cant we hear nowadays.
For of course it is *the sense of the Bible* which is the Bible,
and the question which had to be settled was, What is
the sense of the Bible on this point ?   Scripture and the
primitive Church teach that our Lord is not a creature
but God, that is the central fact of the Christian religion.
Everything else follows, but in order to find a word out
of which the Arians could not wriggle, Athanasius and
his friends fought for one which is not Scriptural or
primitive, but which sums up the Scriptural and primitive
teaching on the point—*homoousion*, " of the same substance with "—and they carried the day.   With the
help of this word the Council defined the Catholic Faith
and banished Arius;   but afterwards a large body of
moderates who had assented to the definition came to
think it had been inexpedient.   Can't we hear them ?—
nice, good old things.   "All this trouble could have been
avoided if the poor dear Archdeacon had been content
with a Scriptural word.   We were getting on so nicely
until he forced upon us that unfortunate word
homoousion."   The importance of the word is best
summed up in a quotation from James Anthony Froude.
" In speaking of Gibbon's work to me, Carlyle," says
Froude, " made one remark which is worth recording.
In earlier years he had spoken contemptuously of the
Athanasian controversy—of the Christian world torn
to pieces over a diphthong, and he would ring the
changes in broad Annandale on *homoousion*, the Catholic
symbol, and the *homoiousion* (of like substance) the Arian
symbol.   He told me now that he perceived Christianity

itself to have been at stake. If the Arians had won it would have dwindled away into a legend."

That, then, was what Athanasius did and stuck to; now see what he suffered for doing it and sticking to it. When noble, gentle, old Archbishop Alexander died, Athanasius was away from Alexandria, but the Archbishop kept murmuring, " He cannot escape, he cannot escape." And he could not. He became Archbishop of Alexandria.

He had three years of peace, during which his diocesan and theological work flourished. Then the battle began. Constantine asked Athanasius to re-instate Arius, and he said, " No, certainly not." Then Eusebius of Nicomedia, an Arian Archbishop who hated Athanasius, got Constantine to issue a mandate to compel Athanasius to restore Arius. Athanasius again said, " No, I won't."

Catholicism was too strong a force to be attacked directly, so the Arians tried to undermine Athanasius. They charged him, first, with arrogating to himself State authority : this was disproved. Then they charged him with subsidizing a rebel : this was disproved. Then came the story of the broken chalice. There was a certain schismatic priest called Ischyras, who had set up a chapel and defied the Archbishop. The Archbishop sent an official to serve an inhibition on him, and the priest was induced to declare that this emissary of Athanasius had thrown the chalice off the altar in the middle of Mass, breaking the chalice and spilling the Precious Blood. This was disproved, and the priest made to confess the lie, but the story cropped up over and over again, and many continued to believe it.

Then the Arians induced a bishop named Arsenius to hide himself away. When he had disappeared they announced that Athanasius had killed Arsenius and cut up his body for magical purposes; in proof they exhibited a dead hand in a box. Athanasius sent out search parties, who played a game of "hunt-the-slipper" with the Arians for some time before they pounced upon the concealed Arsenius.

Meanwhile the Emperor had summoned a Council to investigate the charges against Athanasius. After a time the Council arrived at the charge of murdering Arsenius, and the dead hand was laid upon the table. The Archbishop asked: "How many people knew Arsenius by sight?" A score of hands went up. The Archbishop left the hall and returned leading a veiled figure. Amid dead silence he raised the veil. "Is this Arsenius?" It could not be denied. "Hold out your right hand." Arsenius did so. "Now your left hand." Arsenius did so. Athanasius pointed at the dead hand on the table and surveyed the Court. "I presume you do not think the Almighty gave Arsenius three hands, do you?"

But the Council announced that it would recognize the Arians who were prepared to sign the Catholic formulas, and it censured Athanasius. Athanasius went straight off to Constantinople with five suffragans, and one day when the Emperor went out riding, they lined up across the road and would not let him pass till Athanasius had had a talk with him. The Emperor was getting very sick of the whole matter, but the Archbishop impressed him for the moment.

Then the Arians played another card. They said the

Archbishop was plotting to produce a famine in Constantinople by forbidding the Egyptian corn ships to trade there. At this the Emperor lost his temper; somehow or other Athanasius was the biggest stirrer up of strife in the Empire. He banished him to Belgium.

During his two and a half years at Treves Constantine died, and the three Emperors among whom the Empire was divided called Athanasius back. There were great rejoicings at Alexandria. But at once the attack began again, and the Archbishop was charged with misappropriating the corn sent in charity from Constantinople to the widows of Egypt. Athanasius cleared himself, but the Emperor Constantius had by this time fallen under the influence of the Arian Eusebius. He consented to an Arian Archbishop being consecrated and intruded into the See of Alexandria, and Athanasius went to Rome and laid his case before Pope Julius. He was now in exile again for three years, during which time the Arians got a Council together at Antioch, which confirmed the deposition of Athanasius from his see, and the Pope summoned a Council at Rome, which acquitted Athanasius and condemned the Arian Archbishop Gregory. Councils also met at Milan and Sardica and supported Athanasius.

Then the intruding Archbishop was killed in a civil outbreak as a result of his extraordinary cruelties. The Emperors begged Athanasius to return. He returned with solemn deliberation, visiting the Emperors and getting recognition from church after church on his way. There were overwhelming rejoicings at Alexandria.

Athanasius once more had three years' peace. Then began the worst period of the struggle. The Emperor

Constantius set himself to Arianize the Church. For the time, the Empire became an Arianizing propaganda. There was much persecution of Catholics, and portions of the Church were terrorized into Arianism. The Arian hatred of Athanasius as the arch-Catholic rose to fever heat. Fresh charges of high treason were brought against him, and the great attack was made on his person during an all-night vigil in the Church of St. Theonas.

You remember the story. The roaring mob of soldiery attacked the great doors, but Athanasius ascended to his throne in the apse. " I sat down on the throne," writes the Archbishop, " and commanded the Deacon to chant the Psalm and give thanks unto the Lord for his goodness, and the people to respond, ' For His mercy endureth for ever.' "

Presently the soldiers, clashing their arms and discharging their arrows, rushed into the church. The faithful cried to Athanasius to save himself.

" I am the last man out," shouted the Archbishop; " let the lay folk depart and the monks continue the prayers."

The soldiers had almost reached the throne when the monks whipped the slender Archbishop up in their arms, and fled with him through a hidden passage in the darkness.

The Emperor handed over Alexandria to the Arians, and installed George of Cappadocia, an atrocious scoundrel, as Archbishop. For six years Athanasius was in the desert, hunted from cave to cave, keeping up relations all the while with the Catholics of Alexandria.

All this while he worked hard at theology, and wrote

books as though he were in his library, quite composed and concentrated. Let us contemplate the saint bending over his work hour after hour under the shade of some rock in the scorching desert, and feel ashamed of our own faithless restlessness. Then the Arian Constantius died, the pagan Julian succeeded him, and the pagans of Alexandria rose and killed George, the evil Cappadocian. This time Athanasius could not return in triumph, but one morning somebody went into the library of the Archbishop's house and sprang back with terror; the Archbishop, who had not been seen for six years, was calmly writing a letter at his writing-table. But he did not stay long. " Of all the Christians," said the advisers of Julian, "Athanasius is the most dangerous." Athanasius received a warning to depart, the clergy wept, but the Archbishop smiled. "A passing cloud," he said, and went off up the Nile.

It must have appeared to the Christians as though Paganism were now coming back for a long time. No doubt the Archbishop was in great danger. Once when a government boat in pursuit of him was known to be creeping up upon the boat in which he lay hid, his boatmen were driven to the expedient of turning and rowing at full speed the other way. They were stopped and hailed.

" Is Athanasius far ahead ? " said the officials.

" He is close by," shouted the Archbishop's men, and so got him past.

But Julian died on the 26th June, 363, the cloud passed, and Athanasius returned once more and ruled his diocese for another ten years. Perhaps this is the grandest period of all, for he slipped back into the steady routine of an ordinary Archbishop. He did the prosaic tasks of every day with the same simple perseverance with which he had confessed the Faith through his many exiles and trials. Meanwhile his theological activity never ceased. He dealt with a series of questions of debate as they arose, and gradually drew near to a happy death amid the love and sorrow of his people. He chose his successor, and then, as St. Gregory of Nazianzus says, he ended his life in a holy old age and went to keep company with his fathers—the Patriarchs, Prophets, Apostles and Martyrs, who had fought valiantly for the Faith as he had done.

THE RELIGION OF DR. JOHNSON

In our visions of Dr. Johnson he is generally dining or drinking tea in agreeable company. We may recall, as typical, the great occasion when he was entrapped into meeting his pet aversion, Mr. Wilkes, at the table of Mr. Dilly, the publisher. " ' Who is the gentleman in lace, sir ? ' ' Mr. Wilkes, sir.' This information confounded him, he had some difficulty to restrain himself, but the cheering sound that dinner is upon the table dissolved his reverie, and we all sat down without any symptoms of ill-humour. Mr. Wilkes placed himself next to Dr. Johnson, and behaved to him with so much attention and politeness that he gained upon him insensibly. No man ate more heartily than Johnson, or loved better what was nice and delicate. Mr. Wilkes was very assiduous in helping him to some fine veal. ' Pray, give me leave, sir, it is better here, a little of the brown—some fat, sir. A little of the stuffing. Some gravy. Let me have the pleasure of giving you some butter. Allow me to recommend a squeeze of this orange or the lemon, perhaps, may have more zest.' ' Sir, sir, I am obliged to you,' cried Johnson, bowing and turning his head to him with a look for some time of surly virtue, but in a short while of complacency."

But there is another series of scenes on the significance of which I propose to make some comment. It is Holy

Week, and he is making his anxious, troubled, yearly self-examination before Easter Communion, which he closes with the sigh—this is not the life to which Heaven is promised. And now, his own self-examination finished, he and his black servant, Frank Barber, are kneeling together, and he is helping the boy to do what he himself has just been doing. It is Good Friday, and Boswell, bland, inquisitive, chattering, has invaded him for breakfast; but the old Doctor eats no food, and contents himself with a cup of tea without milk or sugar. Presently they go to St. Clement Danes to service, and at the words in the Litany—in the hour of death and in the day of judgment—Boswell is startled by the tremulous earnestness of his response, "Good Lord, deliver us."

There is no dinner on this day, but between morning and afternoon service Dr. Johnson endeavours to employ himself earnestly in devotional exercises. "He gave me," says Boswell, naïvely, "Pascal's *Pensées*, that I might not interrupt him."

He goes to bed with his fast unbroken, and maintains the same seclusion on Holy Saturday, though in the middle of the day he staves off faintness by eating some cakes and drinking some coffee.

It is Easter Day, and he is in the crowd at Easter Communion, making his ponderous way—sadly deaf and sadly blind—from pew to pew towards the altar, and having regained his place he seats himself as is customary, but thinking the posture to be unfitting, rises and remains standing to the end—conspicuous but unconscious.

And we recall three illustrations of the translation of

this religion into practice. He notes the first in his religious journal. It is the death of an old family servant, Catherine Chambers, that he describes, " my dear old friend," as he calls her.

" I asked all to withdraw, and then told her that we were to part for ever, and that as Christians we should part with prayer, that I would, if she were willing, say a short prayer. She expressed great desire, and held up her poor hands with great fervour while I prayed. I then kissed her. She told me that to part was the greatest pain that she had ever felt, and that she hoped we should meet again in a better place. I expressed, with swelled eyes and great emotion of tenderness, the same hope. We kissed and parted, I humbly hope to meet again to part no more." The second is classical, he told it at Lichfield, a short time before his death. " Once I was disobedient, as a boy, to my father; I refused to attend him to Uttoxeter market. (Michael Johnson was a bookseller and had a bookstall in the market.) Pride was the source of that refusal and the remembrance of it was painful. A few years ago (he must have been about seventy) I desired to atone for this fault. I went to Uttoxeter in very bad weather and stood for a considerable time bare-headed in the rain, on the spot where my father's stall used to stand. In contrition I stood, and I hope the penance was expiatory."

The third story is told by Boswell.

" Coming home late one night he chanced upon a poor woman lying in the street so much exhausted that she could not walk. He took her up in his arms and carried her to his house, where he discovered her to be a prostitute of the lowest grade, who had fallen into the worst state of vice, poverty and disease. Instead of upbraiding her, he had her taken care of with all tenderness for a long time, at a considerable expense, until she was cured; then he tried to put her into a virtuous way of living."

It was in his undergraduate days at Pembroke College, Oxford, that Johnson began to be a religious man. Born of Tory High Church parents he was baptized on the day of his birth, learnt his collect by reading it through twice, while still in petticoats, and was confined to the house on Sundays by his mother, and made to read *The Whole Duty of Man.*

" From a great part of it I could derive no instruction," he says, " and Sunday was a heavy day for me."

When he was three years old, Sacheverell, the popular preacher of Queen Anne's day, came to Lichfield, and a neighbour, meeting Michael Johnson in the dense crowd before the cathedral pulpit, with three-year-old Sam perched upon his shoulder and gaping at Sacheverell, rebuked him for bringing his baby into such a press. Johnson replied that it was impossible to keep Sam at home. He had caught the public feeling for Sacheverell and would have stayed for ever in the church, satisfied with beholding him. But at nine years of age the early piety of Sam abated. The family pew happened to be shut up for repairs, and Sam was too shy, awkward and short-sighted to go and look for a seat in a strange church, so he used to go and read in the fields on Sunday. This went on till fourteen. The family pew must have been re-opened and available, but Sam was still reluctant to go to church. He began to talk loosely against religion, though not, he afterwards remembers, to think much against it. Then, after a while, he went to Oxford, where he says no talk against religion was permitted. One day in Pembroke he took up William Law's *Serious Call to a Devout Life*, expecting to find it dull or ludicrous, but he says, " It over-matched me." In fact, it was the means of his conversion.

Johnson's discussion of the foundations of religion is naturally limited by the arguments of his age. In the eighteenth century, reason contemplating design in Nature inferred necessarily, as it thought, an Intelligent First Cause. Religion, viewed apart from Revelation, meant to the eighteenth century a reasonable account of things, a guide for prudence. In Johnson's day a meagre Natural Religion appears to be securely based upon the evidence of physical nature, so securely that the importance of Christianity as an addition to this was very largely called in question. Nature and Natural Religion were put in array against Christianity to challenge its usefulness.

All objections to religion, Johnson reminds us, cannot be answered. We have demonstration, he says, of a First Cause, good as well as powerful, because there is nothing to make Him otherwise, and goodness is of itself preferable. Yet against this there is what is very certain, the unhappiness of human life. This gives us reason to hope for a future state of compensation and a perfect system. But of that mankind is not sure until there is a positive Revelation (by which he means Christianity). Reasoning *a priori* he admits that there are more arguments against than for some of the Christian facts which appear strange to reason in some degree—

but testimony has great weight and casts the balance. The natural history of testimony he does not seem to have reviewed. A modern objector would retort that the power of accurate observation is of more recent date than the account of the Christian facts. But the wish to believe had led Johnson, conscientious even to scruple, to weigh the counter-arguments with care. " Everything Hume has advanced against Christianity had passed through my mind," he says, " long before he wrote." He admits the force of Hume's dictum " that it is more probable that the witnesses should be mistaken than the miracles true," and the need of great caution in accepting a miracle. His belief in the New Testament miracles he bases first on belief in a personal moral God maintained on other grounds; on the extraordinary practical efficiency of the religion of which they are alleged to be an integral part; on the disinterestedness of the witnesses, and their zeal to the death; on the heathen failure to explode them, and reference of them to diabolic agency; and on the corroborative evidence of the whole trend of previous history. Granted the possibility of miracle, he concludes, we have as strong evidence for the miracles of the New Testament as the nature of the thing admits. Hume, he adds, once admitted to a Durham clergyman that he had never read the New Testament with attention. Boswell has been dipping into Jonathan Edwards and playing with the problem of necessity and freedom. In reply to his proposition, " We are actuated by a series of motives we cannot resist," Johnson's " adamantine common sense "falls back upon the experience of freedom. " You are surer that you are free than you are of prescience, surer you can

lift your finger as you please than of any conclusion
from a deduction of reasoning. All theory is against
the freedom of the will, all experience for it." Boswell
brings up the problem of evil. Johnson declines to be
tempted into a consideration of possible worlds. He
dwells upon the place of moral choice in the scheme of
things which we know. " With all the evil a man would
rather be a free agent than a mere machine without the
evil. If a man would rather be a machine I cannot
agree with him—he is a different being from me."

In considering the elements in a man's personal
religion we have not merely to count them up, we have
to estimate the size of the part which each contributes
to the whole. By far the largest part of Johnson's
religion was his sense of personal responsibility to a
Divine Judge. This, notwithstanding a considerable
personal courage and a singular contempt for pain,
overcast his whole life with a fear of death. " I never
have a moment," he says, " in which death is not terrible
to me." No one was ever more impressed by the fact
that diligence and a right direction of talents is daily
required of men by God. He is constantly composing
prayers, uttering ejaculations, and making resolutions
to a more religious application to duty in face of a final
judgment. This situation is complicated by what he
calls the evident fact of original sin, the evident fact
that men are corrupt, from which complication a way
out has been found on God's part in the Atonement,
on man's part by repentance and obedience. To
Johnson's way of thinking, in the Atonement God
clears Himself by making sufficiently known His perpetual and irreconcilable antagonism to moral evil,

unbars the path of mercy and creates a force which supplies the imperfections of our still necessary obedience, the inefficiency of our still necessary repentance, but such salvation remains conditional on man's fulfilling his part, and no man, as Johnson nervously remembers, can be sure that he has complied with the conditions.

The great defect of Johnson's view is a failure to put the person of Christ in the centre of the picture. Christianity, if it is anything, is a relationship with Christ, and the nervous fear of an honest, well-intentioned man disappears in the contemplation of Christ's figure.

There is a charming illustration of what I mean. Johnson was arguing that friendship was not a Christian virtue, because friendship is preferring the interest of a friend to the neglect of others, and Christianity recommends universal benevolence. Mrs. Knowles, a delightful old Quaker lady, replied: " But especially unto them that are of the household of faith."

" Well, madam, the household of faith is wide enough."

" But, Doctor, our Saviour had twelve disciples, yet there was one whom He loved, the disciple whom Jesus loved."

Johnson's eyes sparkled with pleasure and approval. " Very well, indeed, madam ; you have said very well."

Boswell chimed in: "A fine application. Pray, sir, had you ever thought of it ? "

" I had not, sir."

His attitude towards Holy Communion reveals the same failure: he does not seem to have communicated, as a rule, more than once a year. It is not easy to discover what his belief is about the gift received in the Blessed Sacrament, but it is plain that in relation to the

Blessed Sacrament as in all else our Lord is to him the awful Redeemer, whose redemption is of avail only to those who have conformed themselves to a strict way of living. Communion being required by the Redeemer as part of His system, Johnson obeys every Easter Day with many fears and quakings, after long fasting, self-examination, confession and resolution to amend. He had a profound belief in the efficacy of prayer. "We have the consent of all nations for it," he says, "and Revelation has told us it will be effectual." His practice of daily prayer was steady, prolonged, concentrated, and most devout. He appears to have sometimes made a day's Retreat. He had a rule if he missed one of his two Sunday services to go to church on some day in the following week. Sunday, he used to say, should not be kept with rigid severity and gloom, but with a gravity and simplicity of behaviour. It should be different from any other day. "People may walk, but not throw stones at birds." His rule was (i) to retire early on Saturday night and rise early on Sunday. (ii) To use some special devotion in the morning. (iii) To make a self-examination of his conduct during the past week, and generally to review the course of his life. (iv) To read the Bible on some fixed plan with commentaries and some theological books in addition. (v) To go to church twice. (vi) To give some religious teaching to his household. (vii) To wear off by meditation any worldly soil contracted in the week.

Johnson thought much of an unseen world. At his wife's death, he prayed that if it were possible she might be allowed to minister to him in the spirit state. Prayer for her departed soul and the soul of his departed rela-

171

tions and friends was a settled feature of his devotional
life. " So far as it may be lawful in me, I commend,
O Lord, to Thy Fatherly goodness the soul of my
departed wife, beseeching Thee to grant her whatever
is best in her present state, and finally to receive her to
eternal happiness." In later years he seems to have
prayed without the querying clause, but he felt the
limitation of our knowledge about the future and shrank
from definite statements.

The Parable of Dives and Lazarus, he says, seems to
teach that the souls of the saved do not arrive at once at
the utmost perfection of which they are capable. " I do
not imagine," he said, one starlit night at Ashbourne,
" that all things will be made clear to us immediately
after death, but the ways of Providence will be explained
to us very gradually." He does not gather from St.
Paul's doctrine of the Resurrection of the Body more than
that identity of person will be distinguished. By that
I imagine he means that the spirit will be clothed upon
with a spiritual form having some real relation to what
it has made of its previous fleshly body. He took a
great interest in alleged spirit phenomena and often
discussed them. He recognized that the possibility of
such phenomena follows on any view of the nature of
the human spirit other than that it is merely a name for
some of the operations of the physical organism. He
usually found himself in an atmosphere of incredulity,
expressing itself in bad arguments. His combative
instincts were roused, and he was often on the side of
the ghosts, but never, I think, with a very strong con-
viction that there was good evidence for any particular
instance.

Boswell says of him that no one more strongly demanded a sufficient ground for a belief than Johnson, but he had an intolerance of what Mr. Andrew Lang has called the credulity of the incredulous. This same combative instinct and intolerance of ignorant undiscerning criticism, and of false argument, together with a filial love of all that is of the essence of historical Christianity, often led him to champion Roman Catholicism against the smug Protestantism of his period. He would sometimes talk so vigorously in support of Catholic, and even distinctively Roman doctrine, that old Mr. Langton, Bennet Langton's father, went to the grave believing Johnson to be a Papist. Here is one of the conversations on this subject. Boswell has hired a Bohemian servant—a Roman Catholic. Can he take a Roman Catholic to Scotland ?

J.   If *he* has no objection, sir, *you* can have none.

B.   So, sir, you are no great enemy to the Roman Catholic religion ?

J.   No more, sir, than to the Presbyterian religion.

B.   You are joking.

J.   No, sir, I really think so. Nay, sir, of the two, I prefer the Popish.

B.   How so, sir ?

J.   Why, sir, the Presbyterians have no Church, no Apostolic succession.

B.   And do you think that absolutely essential, sir ?

J.   Why, sir, as it was an Apostolic Constitution, I think it dangerous to be without it. And, sir, the Presbyterians have no public worship. They go to hear a man pray, and are to judge whether they will join with him.

B. But, sir, their doctrine is the same with that of the Church of England. Their confession of Faith and the Thirty-Nine Articles contain the same points, even the doctrine of Predestination.

J. Why, yes, sir, predestination was a part of the clamour of the times, so it is mentioned in our Articles, but with as little positiveness as could be.

B. Is it necessary, sir, to believe all the Thirty-Nine Articles ?

J. Why, sir, that is a question which has been much agitated. Some have thought it necessary that they should all be believed ; others have considered them to be only Articles of peace ; that is to say, you are not to preach against them.

B. What do you think, sir, of Purgatory as believed by the Roman Catholics ?

J. Why, sir, it is a very harmless doctrine. They are of opinion that the generality of mankind are neither so obstinately wicked as to deserve everlasting punishment nor so good as to be admitted into the society of blessed spirits, and therefore that God is graciously pleased to allow of a middle state where they may be purified by certain degrees of suffering. You see, sir, there is nothing unreasonable in this.

B. The idolatry of the Mass ?

J. Sir, there is no idolatry in the Mass. They believe God to be there and they adore Him.

B. The worship of Saints ?

J. Sir, they do not worship Saints; they invoke them; they only ask their prayers. I am talking of the *doctrines* of the Church of Rome. I grant you in practice purgatory is made a lucrative imposition, and that the people do become idolatrous. The worship of images was never inculcated, but it was knowingly permitted in the Middle Ages. I think their giving the Sacrament in one kind is criminal, because it is contrary to the express institution of Christ, and I wonder how the Council of Trent admitted it.

B. Confession?

J. Why, I do not know but that is a good thing. The Scripture says, confess your sins one to another, and the priests confess as well as the laity. Their absolution is only on repentance.

All Johnson's affinities, it is clear, were with this side, though he was the staunchest Church of England man.

During his one visit to Paris he lived with the English Benedictines, and was exceedingly happy in their house. " They treated me very kindly, sir," he said, " and I have a cell appropriated to me in their convent." " I have thought of retiring to a monastery," he said another day, " and have talked it over with a friend, but I find my vocation is rather to active life. I never read of a hermit but in imagination I kiss his feet. Never of a monastery but I could fall on my knees and kiss the pavement." He rightly considers flight from temptation no proper motive for entering a convent. " I said to an Abbess in France, ' Madam, you are not here from love of virtue, but from fear of vice.' She said she would remember this as long as she lived." Poor abbess, one can well believe it.

Johnson's hatred of Presbyterianism was, I imagine, part of the result of his deplorable distaste for all things Scottish.

"Pray, sir," said poor Boswell one day, "can you trace the cause of your antipathy to the Scotch ? "

"I cannot, sir."

"Old Sheridan says it is because they sold Charles I."

"Then, sir, old Sheridan has found out a very good reason."

"People ascribe to you sir, strange sayings. As an instance, that you said you would stand before a battery of cannon to restore the Convocation to its full powers." "Little did I apprehend," says Boswell, "that he had actually said this, but with a determined look he thundered out, 'And would I not, sir ? Shall the Presbyterian Kirk of Scotland have its general assembly and the Church of England be denied its Convocation ? ' His eyes flashed with indignation."

I am afraid he was often very rude in Scotland. When Principal Robertson took him to see St. Giles's, Edinburgh, "Let me see," said he, "what was once a church." The ruins of St. Andrews enraged him. Boswell asked where John Knox was buried. "I hope in the highway," roared Johnson. "I have been looking at his Reformations." He kept his hat off on the ruined site. Some steeple in St. Andrews was in danger. "Don't pull it down, it may fall," said he, "upon some of the posterity of John Knox, and no great matter." Dinner was happily announced. "Aye, aye," said the old fellow, "amid all these sorrowful scenes I have no objection to dinner." He refused to join in Presbyterian worship. Somebody wished him to hear Principal Robertson preach. "I'll hear him," he said, "if he'll get up into a tree and preach, but I will not give a sanction by my presence to a Presbyterian assembly."

Methodism was not organized in Dr. Johnson's day into a series of sects. He had small sympathy with the excitement of the movement. "But the Methodists have done good," he said. "They have spread religious impressions among the vulgar, and I cannot doubt the sincerity of the man who travels nine hundred miles in the month and preaches twelve times in a week." He preferred Wesley to Whitefield. "Whitefield means sincerely well," he said, "but has a mixture of politics and ostentation, whereas Wesley thinks of religion only."

"I talked," says Boswell, "of the recent expulsion of six students from Oxford, who were Methodists, and would not desist from public praying and exhorting."

J. That expulsion was extremely just and proper. What have they to do at a University who are not willing to be taught, but will presume to teach. Where is religion to be learned but at a University? Sir, they were examined and found to be mighty ignorant fellows.

B. But was it not hard, sir, to expel them, for I am told they were good beings?

J. I believe they might be good beings, but they were not fit to be in the University of Oxford. A cow is a very good animal in a field, but we turn her out of a garden.

To the Church of England Johnson had an enthusiastic devotion. "I put him in mind," said Boswell, "when he was in Scotland, that Episcopals were but Dissenters there."

"Sir," said he, "we are here as Christians in Turkey."

And yet his conversation sometimes betrays the fallen state of the English Church. One day he said that condemned criminals were not likely to be impressed by the clergy, and should be attended by a Methodist preacher or a Popish priest.

He is at the level of his age when he writes to Boswell, " If Dean Percy can be popular at Carlisle, he may be very happy. He has in his disposal two livings, each equal, or almost equal, in value to the Deanery. He may take one himself and give the other to his son."

Boswell inserts as very edifying a letter Johnson wrote to a young clergyman in which this admirable advice occurs : " Take care to register the authors from whom your discourses are borrowed. Attempt from time to time an original sermon." Johnson's profound reverence for the hierarchy made him expect from bishops the highest degree of decorum. He was offended even at their going to taverns. "A bishop," said he, " has nothing to do with a tippling house, where he may meet low company." Being once in company with several clergymen who assumed a jolly laxity, he sat grave and silent. At last, and by no means in a whisper, he said, " This merriment of parsons is mightily offensive."

.   .   .   .   .   .

We have passed from graver to lighter aspects of the religious side of Johnson. All that was noblest and deepest in the man shone out at his death. A priest used to come and recite the daily office with him when he lay painfully dying of his dropsy: the last time he asked for only the Litany, and his deep voice uttered the responses with the most profound devotion that can be imagined. He spoke long and earnestly with his friends of religion, of its infinite consequence. The day came when he asked his doctor to tell him plainly of his state.

" You cannot recover," said Dr. Brocklesby, " except by a miracle."

" Then," said Johnson, " I will take no more physic, not even my opiates, for I have prayed that I may render up my soul to God unclouded."

All his fear of death was calmed and absorbed by the prevalence of his faith and his trust in the merits and propitiation of Jesus Christ. He fashioned and uttered a special prayer before receiving his last Communion, " Viaticum," as he was used to call it. After receiving Viaticum he remained in perfect peace and contentment, gradually sinking. On the day of his death a young girl, the daughter of an old friend, came and asked to see him that she might get his blessing. The old Doctor turned himself towards her and said, " God bless you, my dear."

They were his last words. About seven in the evening, Frank Barber, his black servant, sat looking into the fire, lost in thought. Suddenly it struck him that there was a great silence in the room. He ran to the bed and bent over his old master. Johnson was dead.

Men of the Catholic Movement

CHARLES LOWDER

" These are spots in your feasts of charity."—Jude v. 12.

THE year is 1840. The scene is St. Mary's, Oxford, and it is a quarter to five on a Sunday afternoon in term time. The church is packed with people, among them hundreds of undergraduates.

The Vicar of St. Mary's is standing in the pulpit wearing his black gown, and he has just announced this text from St. Jude, in those low, silvery tones which no hearer ever forgot : " These are spots in your feasts of charity." Mr. Newman, in whose mind the argument of Tract XC is at this time taking shape, has been reflecting during the past week on the dangers attending a religious movement.

Amid a breathless stillness, he unfolds his subject in a series of short paragraphs, exquisitely enunciated, with those strange pauses between them which his listeners had come to find part of his charm. " A danger of the present time," said Mr. Newman, " arises from what may be called the luxury of religion. None can rejoice more than the preacher at the increased regard to ecclesiastical architecture and music, and to the ornamenting of our churches. But it must be reflected that these require to be accompanied by personal holiness, and even the spirit of devotion may become little better than a luxurious pleasure unless we maintain a spirit of self-denial in it, and remind ourselves that even devotion must not be so much a gratification to ourselves as a sacrifice to God."

If the preacher, unconsciously drawn by some magnetic attraction, had raised his eyes from his manuscript (a thing Mr. Newman rarely did) he might have met the eager gaze of a tall, handsome, fair-haired boy with a radiant face, shining among the rest because so very few youths have radiant faces. For Mr. Newman had done a great thing with that short paragraph. He had founded St. Peter's, London Docks.

Charles Lowder, the son of a well-to-do banker of Bath, had just come up to Exeter and was enjoying Oxford enormously. He had taken up rowing, and as he had tremendous spirits, charming manners, and was extremely good-looking, he was very popular. He had always taken a keen interest in public affairs. He had been sent to school at the age of nine, and his first letter home runs thus :

" My dear Mamma,

" I like Mr. Simms very well. He wears a gown. We are to learn Caesar and Greek Delectus, and to read Goldsmith's *History of Rome.* O'Connell is to sit in Parliament."

We are not surprised that this charming young man, whose heart and conscience Mr. Newman had awakened, flung himself with enthusiasm on the Tractarian side when Dr. Pusey's Eucharistic teaching was condemned, and he was suspended without a hearing. Charles became a keen Tractarian, and made up his mind to take orders.

While Lowder was at Oxford, his father's bank failed, and he found himself impoverished. He took this with amazing dignity, sweetness and unselfishness. The boy was through and through sterling gold. He got a second in Greats, tried for a fellowship, in which he was beaten by Coleridge (afterwards Lord Chief Justice), and was ordained to a curacy and tutorship in Somersetshire.

Here he met the second great influence in his life, his fellow-curate, Merriman, afterwards Bishop of Grahamstown. Merriman was a missionary by vocation, and he interpreted Lowder to himself. He showed Lowder that the love at his heart was really the love of souls. Lowder tried to go to the mission field, but was prevented by the fact that he had to help the broken fortunes of his family. But the missionary spirit would not rest, and it seized on the work nearest at hand. Lowder got the spiritual charge of the neighbouring workhouse, and set to work at once to teach the older paupers and to improve the schools. He was remembered in his first parish as " the kind young gentleman who used to come and see us very often, and who said the prayers in church every day all by himself."

Picture him, still the radiant boy, on a wet winter morning. He unlocks the damp, old country church, and enters the cold, musty place in the dark. He kindles a candle or two and puts on a surplice, the old square pews stretch around him into the darkness. Above the reading pew rises the tall, gaunt pulpit, which hides the little table doing duty for an altar. The curate has tolled a few strokes on the bell ; no one responds. After a while, the fresh young voice breaks the hollow stillness, and the prayers are recited "to the four walls," as the neighbours said, but really to the most Holy Trinity, and with the angels, the archangels, and the whole company of Heaven. Out of that acorn grew St. Peter's, London Docks.

Then came five years with his family at Tetbury, on the Cotswolds, five years of hard work under the limitations of those days. Tetbury was High Church, but I doubt whether the lowest church in London now has the sort of services Tetbury had in 1846. There were two churches, and each had two celebrations a month.

Lowder taught and taught and taught ; he visited and visited and visited. What people called his beautiful, kind, noble face was seen everywhere. He was often surrounded by the children, and often carrying wild flowers. " Children and flowers," he said, " God made to make the world beautiful." He had the wonderful power with the children which is the gift of purity. He could soothe a crying baby when no one else could. When he went away the children felt that he had taken half the fun with him.

He went in 1851 and began his battle for God at St. Barnabas, Pimlico. Mr. Bennett had just been driven out of his living by the Prime Minister, the Bishop and a Protestant mob. Mr. Liddell had been appointed to St. Paul's, Knightsbridge, and he had installed Mr. Skinner as curate in charge of St. Barnabas.

The clergy of St. Barnabas and the choristers lived then in community as we do at All Saints', Margaret Street. The order, the reverence and the music were of the best.

The Protestant riots had been going on for some time when Lowder arrived. The principal laymen had been sworn in as special constables, and they stood all through the service drawn up at the chancel screen to defend the choir.

The ritual attacked was not the ritual of All Saints', Margaret Street, it was the ritual of St. Paul's Cathedral as it is now. The choir and clergy walking in two and two, the eastward position, cross and flowers on the altar, and coloured frontals for the seasons. The Bishop, to appease the mob, had ordered the cross and flowers off the altar. " I will have that cross removed if it costs me my see," he had said, with the gesture of a Christian martyr. He had stopped the office being sung in the chancel, and had ordered a reading place to be made in the nave. He had forbidden the priest to carry the chalice to the altar, and had characterized the plan of communicating the choir before the congregation as extremely ritualistic.

Nevertheless, the mob still battered on the doors, shouted through the windows, hissed in the aisles and charged the chancel gates. Lowder the junior was solid with his brethren that they must stand firm against this combination of tyrannies, but he was wholly immersed in his work among the poor in horrible slums, which then lay west of Ebury Square, and have since been cleared away.

Lowder was weak in imagination, he had no æsthetic taste or skill. His strength lay in logic and courage. To him ritual was a logical necessity, the employment of a natural law in the service of revelation. Given a human soul and body for the instrument, the Catholic

Creeds for the subject, and Almighty God for the object of faith and worship, then ritual is the only process by which Christian worship can be outwardly paid.

And then, suddenly, the third great influence entered into Lowder's life, and St. Peter's appeared on the horizon.

One day Lowder found the choirboys of St. Barnabas filling their pockets with stones and preparing to bombard a sandwichman who carried a Protestant sandwich board. " You must not hurt that unhappy man," said Charles, " it would be very wrong ; it would not, however, be wrong to obscure the words he is carrying. Throw the stones away, and there is sixpence to buy rotten eggs with." Now, it was the year of the Great Exhibition, and Prince Albert had brought in the reign of plenty. Rotten eggs were very, very cheap that year, and you could get a lovely lot for sixpence. Consequently, the sandwich-board was successfully veiled in greenish yellow, and the Protestant Party complained to the Bishop. The Bishop was secretly rather amused and in private talked of Lowder's " ovation," but publicly he was very indignant and suspended Lowder for six weeks.

Lowder was deeply penitent at having given scandal. His brother said he had never seen anyone so broken-hearted. He went to France for the six weeks, and lived with a group of French clergy, and in France he came face to face with the man who fixed his career.

That man was St. Vincent de Paul, for he began to study the life and methods of St. Vincent, and St. Vincent sent him to London Docks.

At this time there had lived in the East End for fifteen years a depressed clergyman called Bryan King. He was rector of St. George's-in-the-East, a parish of 30,000, through which Ratcliff Highway ran. The parallelogram in which the church stood contained 735 houses, of which 40 were public houses and 154 houses of ill-fame. Many of these houses did a combined trade. Ratcliff Highway and its surroundings sheltered the scum of all Europe. There is no plague spot so bad as this in London to-day. Lowder and a little group of priests, all inspired by the example of St. Vincent de Paul, offered to give what help they could to Bryan King.

So one evening Lowder and a friend went down to a room in a court off Ratcliff Highway, and somebody rang a bell at the entrance of the court, and two or three of Mr. Bryan King's decent old women came, and nobody else.

A fortnight afterwards they tried another pitch in the worst alley in the neighbourhood. Here they were attacked by Irish Roman Catholics with wild fury. There were no stones handy, so the Irish smashed up a beer pitcher and pelted the priests with the pieces. The uproar went on for a week or two. Then the Irish got tired of it and stopped—but nobody came to listen. Lowder's companions began to drop off.

" Will you also go away? " said Bryan King to Lowder.

" On the contrary," said Lowder, " I shall come and stay."

They took a hideous and horrible old house left derelict in the slums, and made it the headquarters of a knot of priests, and so the mission began. Lowder prepared for it by going to the first retreat for priests held in the revival, at Dr. Pusey's house in Christ Church.

Lowder arrived on the scene in 1856. St. Peter's, London Docks, was consecrated in 1866. Lowder died in 1880. The twenty-four years were given to ceaseless labour for the salvation of souls in the worst quarter in London, and the building up of a devout Christian community of the souls thus saved. This work was helped greatly by the call to fight two terrible enemies, the attack of organized evil in 1860, under the guise of Protestantism, in the St. George's riots, and the epidemic of Asiatic cholera in 1866.

In considering Lowder's work, mark in what his power lay. He had no outstanding personal gifts, he was a poor preacher with a difficult manner ; although the children liked having him better than anybody else, he did not catechise particularly well ; the strain of his work made him seem cold and restrained to the people he worked with ; naturally excitable, he had so schooled himself to self-restraint that his friends said that it was not until his bodily health weakened that the love within him could break through this self-denying ordinance, and shine forth at all times.

No, Lowder's power was simply the power of a human will entirely given to the salvation of souls for the glory of God ; that was the power with which he applied the instrument of the Catholic Religion, and worked the miracle of London Docks.

He was marvellously tender with the sick ; in illustra-tion they sketch him ministering to the body as well as the soul of a woman dying of typhus. He was marvellously tender to the fallen : he established rescue homes for the poor girls he brought to the Sisters from the dens he found them in. A Sister describes his arrival once in the middle of the night with a girl he had saved from throwing herself into the docks. She was raving and struggling in his arms, and the Sister said that the calm love with which he looked down on her made his face shine with light.

On the Cotswolds Lowder had said that God made children to make the world beautiful. It could not be said that the world was made beautiful by the poor children of the docks. Half-naked, stunted, deformed, many half-witted, they lived in a vast brothel in which their parents, their brothers and sisters and themselves were all more or less implicated.

But they came to adore Lowder, and through love he reclaimed them, drew them into Christian schools, and gradually purified their homes and their lives. Lowder often stopped street fights, and for a long stretch of time faced infuriated mobs, but the characteristic picture of him shows him with a band of tinies about him, two or three of whom are spreading out his priest's cloak like a tent while the others struggle to get inside with shouts of laughter ; or he is surrounded by a band of bigger boys and girls all listening with laughing eyes to his funny stories ; or he is stroking a crew of rough lads on the river, and from all sides as they row by comes the cheery shout, "Hulloa, Father Lowder !" Such was the personality and spirit of the missioner, but these alone could not have created the community of Christians who worshipped at St. Peter's, London Docks. The missioner converted these people with the instrument he brought to bear on them, and that instrument was the Catholic Religion.

He showed them his Master, Jesus Christ. He told them to come to Jesus, but he also showed them how to come, and when. He told them that the blood of Jesus cleanseth from all sin, but he also taught them how it is applied. These people came to believe that their children were regenerate in Baptism ; they came to believe that the Holy Ghost is given in Confirmation ; they came to believe that our Lord has left power to His Church to absolve ; they came to believe that the Blessed Sacrament has an inward part, and that it is the Body and Blood of Christ ; they came to believe that there, there on that spot of ground where sin had reigned, there had now come this Power, and had begun to reign ; they transferred their allegiance, and found themselves lifted up into peace and joy.

After five years of this work began the riots at St. George's-in-the-East, in which publicans and brothel-keepers fought our Lord with the weapons of Protestantism. I will not speak of the disgraceful attitude of the Church authorities. I content myself with saying that the police refused protection to the priests as far as they could. Bryan King and his curate broke down, and Lowder and Mackonochie, who came to help him, faced the music. The mob seized the choir stalls, pelted the altar with bread and butter and orange peel, tore down the altar cross, spat on and kicked the clergy. One day they would have thrown Lowder into the docks if his friends had not made a cordon across the dock bridge, and enabled him to get to the Mission House by a back way.

Lowder said that much good came out of this. It was a grand advertisement. The lowest and vilest were made to think about religion. His reply to the riots was to buy the site on which St. Peter's stands to-day.

St. Peter's had just been consecrated when the cholera came. Of all plagues this is the most awful, far worse than bubonic plague or the Black Death. In Asiatic cholera fiends appear to have seized the victim, and to be tearing him in pieces.

In this visitation the Anglo-Catholics won their spurs. Dr. Pusey came down to help, laymen, among them Lord Halifax, came to work with Lowder and his priests. Morning after morning they met for communion in the newly-consecrated St. Peter's, and separated for the appalling labours of the day, each recognizing that the day might be his last.

When at length the cholera vanished, it left Lowder completely master of the field. Nobody wanted to attack him or his methods again.

As he was seen carrying some cholera-stricken child in his arms to the hospital, the people began to call him " Father." Thus was the title " Father " won for the secular clergy of the Anglo-Catholic movement : it is a title which they will only retain as long as they are true to this ideal

My tale is told. After the cholera, Lowder's work lay in holding the field he had won for our Lord.

There came a night, fourteen years after, which had

a significance unrecognized at the time. It was school treat day, and in the evening nineteen large vans crammed within and without with happy, cheering children came home from Epping Forest, and rolled over the dock bridge, Father Lowder in the midst with a baby on each knee.

To their complete surprise they found the whole parish *en fête*, banners and coloured lights decorated all the windows, cheering crowds filled the streets, and the parish band played the Father home.

Six weeks afterwards the over-strain found him out, and he died suddenly on his holiday in the Austrian Tyrol.

Once more the streets are crowded but now by silent crowds. St. Peter's stands open far into the night, and is crowded by the poor. The Masses begin at 3 a.m., hundreds receive Holy Communion. Later in the morning the people go to the confines of the parish to receive the Father's body. It is borne across the bridge which his friends had once held to save his life in the days when the police would not intervene, but now the police are there in reverence to clear a way, for the crowd is thronging round the bier, and trying to lay their loving hands upon the pall made holy by the Father's body.

So they carried his body to his church, and laid it before the altar which he had built with his life's blood.

Those who saw the scene all marked one feature— at every point the crowd was fringed with little children who were crying inconsolably.

So I make my first point. To the morale, that is to say, to the inspiring and controlling spirit of a *true* Anglo-Catholic movement, the first essential is a thirst for souls.

ROBERT RADCLIFFE DOLLING

He stirreth up the people."—*St. Luke* xxiii. 5.

THE year before Charles Lowder went down to preach in Lower Well Alley and was pelted with broken crockery by wild Irish, a little boy lay dying in a big country house in the north of Ireland. It was the boy's fourth birthday, and he asked to see his birthday cake. They brought it to him, and his eyes dwelt on it with satisfaction. " Give everybody in the house a bit," said the weak voice, "and don't forget the people in the kitchen." Having said this, the little boy took a turn for the better, and lived another forty-seven years, during which he was the champion of all the people in the world who live below stairs.

But Bob Dolling's gospel was not the easy gospel of good nature, it was the natural outcome of a direct apprehension of God.

He had recovered, and was sitting again by his mother, eating his dinner with a dessert spoon at the family luncheon. He was now four and a half. A guest began to talk theology with Bob's father and mother and said that he had always found the doctrine of the Trinity a difficulty.

" On my plate," said Bob suddenly, " there are three

196

things, gravy, meat and 'tatoes, but" (with a grin) " they are all one dinner. That's like the Trinity."

Dolling was never a subtle theologian, it must be confessed, to the end of his days. As I have said, he had the mystic's direct personal knowledge of God, and he no more needed a theology to *support* his belief in God than you need an astronomy to support your belief in the sun, moon and stars.

When Bob was seven, he and his younger sister, Josephine, had a terrifying experience. They found themselves perched on an outside car being driven at nightfall through a dark and lonely wood. All woods are terrible at nightfall, but what with banshees and other supernatural Irish beings, whose names I dare not pronounce in public, Irish woods are worse than any, and if there is a type of vehicle from which an ogre could pick you off in a moment it is an Irish outside car.

Bobby felt it was time to do something. " It's all right, Joey," he said, " I am going to pray, then nothing can hurt us. ' Lighten our darkness we beseech Thee, O Lord, and by Thy great mercy defend us from all perils and dangers of this night, for the love of Thine only Son, our Saviour Jesus Christ.' "

Robert Dolling had a very good Protestant father, and a very beautiful Evangelical mother who saturated her children's minds with the Gospel story: but he grew up a Catholic because he saw that Catholicism is the language through which God communicates Himself most fully and most subtly to man. Philosophically Dolling was a pragmatist, a man who believes that utility is the guide to truth ; he was a Catholic because he saw that

Catholicism is the religion which works, he saw in it the expression which God has devised for His message ; and he was so sure of this that he never saw the slightest need for a Papal authority to enforce it, and was extremely impatient when Popes in the guise of English bishops tried to hinder it.

Scott Holland has sketched Dolling's religion, and I will give you Holland's words.

" Religion," says Holland, " after all, must be religion ; it must mean a spiritual life, a converted will, a humble and contrite heart, a love of God and of man. Dolling let nothing overlay these or compensate for the lack of these. He had indeed a certain body of ritual practice, more or less elaborate and very definite in its intention. And he appreciated beautiful ministrations. But the secret of his work lay behind or underneath this.

" He insisted indeed strongly on the Sacrament of Penance and Absolution, but then this was to him an essential element and agent in the process of conversion. He preserved the central dominance over all worship of Eucharistic adoration ; but then the Sacrament of the Altar was to him the spirit and the life. He could not conceive a division between the inward and the outward manifestation of God's pardoning grace. Evangelical and Catholic truth found here for him their perfect fusion, in the hunger of the forgiven soul for the Body and the Blood present in the Bread and the Wine. All this he needed to have emphatic and pronounced, without disguise or modification, if his vivid missionary attack was to be possessed of its obvious completion.

" His inward message could not bear to be deprived of its outward expression, and he was angry at any cautious check put upon him, yet not so much with the Ritualist's ecclesiastical anxiety as with the Missioner's indignation at being thwarted in his Gospel."

Now I must sketch Dolling's life for you.

In Lowder and Dolling we have examples of the two age-long types of men who serve God in this world— the Priest and the Prophet.

The work of the true priest is circumscribed by his times, within their limit he serves God faithfully in the plot of ground assigned to him. In the last chapter we saw Lowder doing this, we saw him get to work on a plague spot and cleanse it.

The office of the prophet is to stand above his times and see further than his contemporaries see. Dolling's mission was to make for the forces which underlay the plague spot and try to reform them ; he found them knit up with the fabric of English society. To attack society at any point is to find oneself up against much honest public opinion. Dolling attacked social evils and suffered accordingly.

Dolling, whose father had considerable estates in the north of Ireland, was an Irishman by birth, but by descent he was French and English. He was educated in England, at a private school where they chiefly remember his hatred of falsehood and cruelty ; at Harrow, where they say his life was chivalrous and unstained : and for a short time at Trinity College, Cambridge, where, his health breaking down and his eyes failing, he could not read for his degree. After a time abroad he returned to Ireland and worked at land agency under his father. During the whole of this time, whenever he was at home, Dolling was a boy missionary to the lads on and round his father's estate, the lads of Kilrea. Master Robert as a little boy, the centre of all the fun at the school treats ; Master Robert's parties for the boys up at the Big House ; Master Robert's night school where he taught reading, writing and arithmetic ; Master Robert's Bible and Prayer Book class on Sundays ; Master Robert's potato patch where the boys planted potatoes, his flower garden which they made out of a plantation ; his library where every boy had to read one evening a week ; his expeditions to the sea, where they swam and sat on the rocks and he told them stories. The charity dances he and his boys and their fiddler gave, at which he and his boys danced half the night to help an old woman pay her rent and buy her pig. And Master Bob's sick visiting, too, when he brought food and dressed wounds ; and his visits to mourners, when Master Bob spoke of our Lord and prayed aloud.

In one place or another, Kilrea, Dublin, London, Portsmouth, and again London, so Dolling lived. He was not ordained until he was thirty-one ; up to then he was, of all odd things, a land agent and a rent collector in Ireland.

But towards the end of this period, whenever he could be in London he was immersed over here in St. Martin's League.

The young Orange land agent had met Arthur Stanton, and had found his ideal in Stanton and the band of five hundred postmen who constituted St. Martin's

League. This was a purely social institution for post-men, with club houses where food, rest and recreation could be obtained.

Dolling had by this time made his first confession, and his Catholicism had become definite and clear in the atmosphere of St. Alban's, Holborn.

To the postmen Dolling was " Brother Bob," and both here and in Dublin which was at this time his headquarters, he helped to carry on Stanton's work, and finally became Warden of the League House in Borough Road.

Dolling was perfectly happy in the liberty, equality and fraternity of the League House in the Borough, so happy that he began to feel that this was surface work and that he must dig deeper. He made friends with the boys of the lowest and roughest class, the hooligans ; they were filthy and in such rags that Dolling called them " the Angels " because their tatters looked like wings. Dolling used to have his kitchen boiler lit and make the boys strip and wash themselves all over ; he fed them and gave them what clothes he could collect. On one Christmas Day he is said to have given the hooligans so good a meat dinner that there was no room for more. Dolling took them for a long run to shake down the first course, then they returned to finish the pudding.

This, I think, corresponds in Dolling's life to the moment when St. Francis kissed the leper. The spruce young postmen very naturally objected ; they said they could not live in an entomological museum.

This convinced Dolling that he had a mission to the verminous, and that he could not fulfil it without the priesthood. He went to Salisbury Theological College where, I need not say, he felt rather uncomfortable, and was ordained to a parish in the Salisbury diocese, which sent him as its missionary to work in an East End district.

Under Bishop Walsham How, Dolling began his characteristic work in the East End of London at Maidman Street, Stepney : he ended his life in the East End at St. Saviour's, Poplar.

But his middle period at St. Agatha's, Landport, was his great period, and it is from this that we must gather his message to the Anglo-Catholic movement to-day.

After Dolling had been two years at Stepney, Bishop Temple ordained him priest, but declined to give him an independent sphere of work.

Our Francis had not found an Innocent III. Bishop Temple was a truly great man, but he was bound by the limitations of his position. Until the Church of England is liberated from State control it can never produce an Innocent III.

At this critical moment Dolling was offered the Winchester College Mission at St. Agatha's, Landport, vacant owing to the promotion of Dr. Linklater, the missioner, to Holy Trinity, Stroud Green.

There is nothing more honourable in recent English Church history than the relations between Dolling and Winchester College.

Winchester stands for the cultured English tradition in its finished completeness. " It had," as Scott Holland says, " the curious type of worship peculiar to the Public Schools, with its ancient prehistoric conditions, unlike anything else on the face of the earth, and its terror of anything that commits it, or of anyone who should let himself go."

" Winchester men were perhaps " (I am still quoting Scott Holland) " of all living beings the most remote from the special form of spiritual work which Dolling embodies." But Winchester recognized the Prophet of God, and this shows us the essential rightness of the true English tradition. Not only did Dolling make the mission a vital part of the daily life of the school and bring the boys to have a personal share and vital pride in it, but both masters and boys drew him into school politics and school secrets, and made him their confidant. They all saw in him their ideal of a religious, God-fearing man.

To Wykehamists, Dolling was Dolling, and in a category all to himself.

" Dolling has been preaching at voluntary chapel all through Holy Week at half-past four in the afternoon," once said a Wykehamist to me.

" How many did he get ? " said I, remembering that like most Holy Weeks it had been gorgeously fine.

" Oh, about four hundred."

St. Agatha's, Landport, as Dolling found it, was like a pirates' nest. Full of the deepest degradation, but a scene of tumult, excitement and loud laughter. Public houses of the lowest class, fifty bad houses, streets full of romping, practical jokes, horse-play ; cheap jacks and round-abouts, and booths on every open space. A Bunyan's Vanity Fair of the lowest class.

For this spot Dolling collected £50,000. Here he built a parsonage big enough to take in the poor, the halt and the blind, a great gymnasium, swimming baths, and a grand basilican church. Here he gathered tramps and thieves and Winchester prefects and soldiers and sailors, and even good Bishop Thorold himself, who, being asked to select his neighbours at dinner, chose the two most accomplished thieves in the party, a party which Dolling made easy by his genial loving-kindness. He closed the fifty brothels, fought the licensing authorities, reduced the public houses, and headed a successful movement for shorter hours in the shops. He made friends with politicians of every hue, and with dissenters of every denomination. When Stewart Headlam had preached Socialism, and the Warden of Winchester had written Dolling an angry letter and Dolling had resigned, the chapels held prayer meetings for him and prayed he might remain, and Winchester hastened to say that the Warden's letter was not official and need not be remembered any more.

A general request from the town that he would reconsider his decision was headed by a leading member of the Primrose League. Dolling and a Baptist minister were the great twin brethren in the public fight with evil.

The fact is that the love of all men which radiated from him, and the utter sincerity and self-sacrifice of his life got him a hearing. When he spoke on the evils which lie beneath the surface of our civilization, men listened because all the while he was curing the ills around him and giving his life-blood to the task.

We come now to the moral of this tale.

A true Anglo-Catholic movement must not be content with remedying examples of evil when it finds them : it must fight wrong and oppression on a large scale.

It must seek to remedy the conditions which maintain social wrong.

Dolling insisted that the Church had a duty to speak on social and political questions. He pointed to the Psalms, he pointed out that the chief idea underlying a great part of the Psalter is the right to the poor to be heard by God and by men in all their needs and necessities and to gain the redress of their wrongs.

He reminds us that the prophets are political and social reformers, heard before kings and throughout the land and even over its borders. These men whose writings form so great a part of the Bible had one purpose, they preached the God of justice, a purpose the execution of which involved a most vigorous onslaught on every kind of oppression, on every species of wrong.

"Our Lord," continues Dolling, "gathers all this up, and comes as the champion of the weak and oppressed. The words for which He was cast out of the synagogue of Nazareth were words of social reform.

"But more—Christ preaches the royalty of every single man. He shows men that there is no height they may not rise to if they are true to the power God has given them.

"But Christ saw that some men have absorbed and monopolized the rights of others and hindered their development and denied them the fulfilment of their destiny. He bids men be free to realize their destiny.

"Hence, if any custom, if any privilege, is denying to men this opportunity, the Christian must never cease to raise his voice until this restriction is removed."

You see then how the message of Dolling, the prophet, is bound to have a wider range than the message of

Lowder, the priest. Dolling had a mission to prophesy against such underlying conditions of society as helped to produce such patches of vice and disorder as he and Lowder dealt with, and he had the right to speak because he was doing the work.

If we are going to lead England forward to a better state of things we must have the grit to work and also the pluck to speak.

For a good English man or woman it is easier to work than to speak. You must borrow from the Celt. In politics, ethics, economics, as a Christian you must make yourself felt.

Is it ever said to-day that on such and such a Borough Council Anglo-Catholics are very strong and are affecting its policy ? Have we begun to be remembered by Parliamentarians as a factor to be counted with ?

Dolling would have this so, and so would the prophets and psalmists of the Bible.

There have been Anglo-Catholic summer schools at Oxford for the study of social questions. What a good thing if you joined one and formed your mind on social problems! I know no autobiography of recent times which has impressed me more than Mrs. Sidney Webb's *My Apprenticeship*. The story of how that wealthy girl in her luxurious home made social questions her concern is one of the finest things I know.

Dolling left London over a dispute with Archbishop Temple. He left Landport over a dispute with Archbishop Davidson. It was about Prayers for the Dead. With a little diplomacy Dolling could have got his way, I fancy, but he was an Irishman, and when he was up against a bishop he could not help trailing his coat. Besides, he felt a principle was at stake. But the sunshine went out of his life then. He became a sadder man.

To-night he has his reward. Everything in the matter of the Faithful Departed for which he fought is conceded in the Revised Prayer Book, and the altar of the Holy Souls, which he was not allowed to erect for Harry Moor in St. Agatha's, has been erected for Lord Kitchener in St. Paul's Cathedral.

It seems a pity and a waste, but no doubt Dr. Johnson was right when he said, " Sir, the only method by which religious truth can be established is by martyrdom."

EDWARD KING

" Beloved, let us love one another, for love is of God, and every one
that loveth is born of God and knoweth God."—1 *St. John* iv. 7.

THE Archdeacon of Rochester rang the bell. Working
in his study after breakfast he had been stung by the
splendour of a sudden thought. He told the servant
who came to send in Master Edward. In due course
Master Edward appeared, and stood looking at his
father with a pair of straight, unswerving, very blue
eyes, a slim, graceful, rather delicate boy with a luminous
look. Scott Holland said that Edward King had just
the sort of face you felt a human being *ought* to have.

" Edward," said the Archdeacon, " I suppose you
know your catechism ? "

" Oh, yes, father."

" Quite well ? "

" Oh, yes, quite well, father."

" I supposed so. Well, my boy, I want you to take
out your pony this afternoon, and ride over to Foots
Cray. The Archbishop is holding a confirmation there,
and we had better take this opportunity of getting you
confirmed; you can put up your pony at the rectory,
and you will take a card from me to the Rector."

" Oh, all right, father, thank you."

The Archdeacon was a most excellent man, his children

were devoted to him, and they all adored their admirable mother ; none of the children at Stone Park would have thought of questioning a parental decision. So after luncheon Edward saddled his pony. He was a capital horseman ; one of the people into whom the spirit of a horse enters when he gets on his back ; to the day of his death he had that instinctive knowledge of a horse which only a few possess. He might have been a great Newmarket trainer.

Behold Edward, therefore, trotting cheerfully through the country lanes towards Foots Cray to be confirmed by Archbishop Howley, who was approaching it more ponderously from Lambeth in his coach and his wig.

The Kings were all going to a dance that evening, but struck, perhaps, by a look in the boy's face at tea-time, his mother said to him, " Edward, would you rather stay at home to-night ? " and Edward said, " Yes, please, mother." So they all went off to the ball, and Edward said his prayers and went to bed in the stillness of the empty house.

Look at Edward as he lies asleep. He is destined to stand before the English Church as the typical embodiment of the Good Shepherd.

Lowder showed us that a true Anglo-Catholic move-ment must have a thirst for souls, and Dolling added that this must bring it into conflict with all the forces which make for oppression and wrong-doing.

Now we come to consider the spirit of this fight-ing force, and at once we see that if it is to fight the Lord Jesus Christ's battle in the Lord Jesus Christ's way, it must see and love the best in all men.

In this chapter I begin with my moral and illustrate my moral from my tale.

What is the Anglo-Catholic Movement out for ? If we asked Bishop King he would answer that it is out to preach the Gospel of the Grace of God manifested in the Incarnation of His Son, and coming with the fulness of the blessing of Christ in His Holy Church ; or to use Bishop King's simple phrase, " To bring to the people of England the blessings of the Church."

Now Cardinal Manning used to say a thing about this work which has always stuck in my mind. He said that all teaching, and therefore this work of ours, is like a game of dominoes ; you do it by trying to meet the number the man opposite to you puts down with the same number.

You see, in teaching a man you want to give him something better than his best. You can only do that by starting with him on the basis of his best, you always have to begin by meeting him on common ground and then taking him up a step higher. To do this you must know where to meet him, you must grasp what aspect of goodness is at present appealing to him, and this can only be done by sympathy, by loving what the man loves, and loving him for loving it.

Does that sound complicated ? It is the simplest thing in the world. You want to be the Lord Christ's messenger to your neighbour ? Very well, to be that, your love must instinctively seize on and love what is lovable in your neighbour.

A truism, you say. If so, the most neglected of all truisms, because, as a matter of fact, the possession of a religious and ethical standard strongly tempts us to think that criticism and not love is our first duty towards those who differ from us.

Incomparably the most grievous sin of Christians is criticism and detraction of others. There is nothing at all which retards the spread of the knowledge and spirit of Christ as that does.

If the natural desire of the minds of Anglo-Catholics was to find beautiful points of agreement with their friends, if they naturally shrank from dwelling on points of difference, if love to their neighbour was natural to them and disagreement with their neighbours, when a moral necessity, a matter which needed the help of supernatural grace, then the whole Anglo-Catholic Movement would be transformed because it would have put on Christ.

Think of our Lord. It was natural to Him to love all men and all things. Form, atmosphere, colour, scent, flowers and children, birds and beasts and fishes, He loved them all and saw in their beauty symbols of all the spiritual beauty which He still discerned in those whom sin and disorder of mind and body had partially wrecked.

Such was our Lord's nature, and the same nature inspired His controversy and His condemnations. They were always His defence of love against that which would injure or destroy it.

Now, if the Anglo-Catholic Movement is a true movement of the Spirit of Christ, this will be its spirit, it will be eagerly sympathetic and loving towards those to whom it goes.

In the main our English people are believers in God the Father and in our Lord ; they are baptized, they hold to the Bible, and they pray. " In all this," said Edward King once, " there is matter for great thankfulness and hope."

Here is our common ground ; we must always begin by joyfully uniting ourselves with our neighbours in holding these precious truths. That is what is meant by " Anglo " in the double word Anglo-Catholic. " Anglo " stands for a recognition and love of what is truly Christian in our English religious tradition, that which makes the basis of an appeal for a wider and deeper Catholicism.

Of the six men I am speaking about, three, Lowder, King and Benson, were disciples of Keble and Pusey, and were devout lovers of the English religious tradition. The other three, Dolling, Stanton and Weston, were disciples in some respects of Frederick Robertson, in others of Hurrell Froude, and were painfully sensitive to the defects in the English religious tradition. But they were all six the passionate lovers of Him who has continued to maintain life in the English tradition, our Lord Jesus Christ, and of the sacred Scriptures which point to Him.

We want both these strains in the Anglo-Catholic Movement. At the source they are one, and both are needed for the proclamation of the full truth.

Now let us look at this figure which shows us the love that draws men to Christ : Edward King.

The Oxford verdict of his undergraduate days was, " King is a royal fellow." And that is the key-word to such as King. This thing we are looking at now is Royalty in Human Nature. His link with his contemporaries was his love of country pursuits. He was an

expert about horses, a good shot and a very keen fisher-
man, with a great love of natural scenery, animals and
flowers. In after life, the interests of the supernatural
world so absorbed him that only love of scenery and
flowers competed with them. But Lord Yarborough
said that when the old Bishop was staying in a country
house, as soon as he got into the stables a look of awed
veneration crept over the faces of the hunting men.
"Uncommon knowin' old bird, the Bishop, jolly good
eye for a gee."

I must in honesty set against these charms the fact
that he never missed College Chapel. This resulted
in the dear old chestnut about Hawkins. Dr. Hawkins,
the terrifying Provost of Oriel, found it his pleasure
and duty to snub all undergraduates at collections.
Edward King in his turn appeared before the semi-circle
of Dons in the senior common room, and the Dean in
clear, metallic tones made his report.

"Mr. King has attended every chapel throughout
the term, Mr. Provost."

"Remember, Mr. King, that even a too regular
attendance at College chapel may degenerate into formal-
ism. Good morning."

King was ordained curate of Wheatley, seven miles
from Oxford, and here the royalty in him which Oxford
had recognized shone out at once. Equally at home
with nobles and ploughboys, he began with ploughboys.
We all love Great Danes and bull terriers, why should
we not love ploughboys? King did, and they loved
him. He was very delicate in those days, and suffered
from his heart a great deal, and the ploughboys used to
pull him up the long hill to Cuddesdon.

"The simple carter lads," he wrote, "require to be surrounded with a constant flame of love, to save them from the hardness which their life with the animals and the rough men brings on them. Our dear country poor—I feel more suited to them than to others— require to be helped one by one ; they are very ignorant, have very little time ; work very hard and often with poor food ; they require a great deal of loving, watchful sympathy."

People say to me, "The religious condition of the country villages is simply appalling." No, it is what Edward King here says it is, and he points us to the remedy. "I never could write to you as if you were a gentleman," one of the Wheatley lads once wrote to King, and that means that he had found the secret of access to their souls. It was love. And what else ? Well, near his big chair in the big window of the palace at Lincoln in which the old Bishop used to sit and look down across the terraces of his garden, there always stood two objects ; one was an ostrich egg, the great treasure of the blacksmith at Wheatley, which he had given to King as a parting present, the other was a box, a perfectly square, plain, wooden box, the parting present of the carpenter. When King had expressed his pleasure the carpenter beamed with satisfaction. "I knew you would like it," he said, "because it is the same on every side."

I remember that of the Heavenly city it is said that the breadth and the length and the height of it are equal, and I imagine that the carpenter had seen in the character of King a quality to which he had assigned a similar symbol.

After five years at Wheatley, King climbed the long Cuddesdon hill, up which his beloved plough boys had dragged him, and became first Chaplain and then Principal of the College. Here he did, I suppose, his greatest work of all. He poured his spirit into the future priests of the Movement, for by this time King had gently blossomed into an Anglo-Catholic, making his first confession in time to be able to help others to make theirs. The result was that the young graduates who came with a good deal of misgiving—" They did not unpack for a fortnight," King used to say—found themselves entering, as they afterwards admitted, upon the most delightful life they had ever experienced.

" The penetration of King's love," says one of them, " went home in each case with such direct personal application that the only course was to submit our lives and difficulties, our temptations and sins, our hopes and fears, to one who seemed to know all about them without needing to be told, and so benefit by the guidance for the future of one who had shown himself clairvoyant of the past."

King kept up with people all his life. Just before he died he wrote to one of the little village boys at Wheatley, now seventy-four years of age, " God bless you, dear Charlie, and guide you on to the end which is really the great beginning. Remember me in your prayers as I do you every day. God bless you and all like you."

And two years before this he had written to an old Cuddesdon student, " Thank you so much for your loving words. ' He loved them to the end.' This is our standard. I was seventy-eight two Sundays ago, so you must keep up your love a little longer, and then in Paradise it will, God willing, be like Cuddesdon again."

There are certain things which must be said about King at this point if you are to get a properly proportioned picture of the man who stands as the typical Good Shepherd of the Anglo-Catholic revival.

You always felt that he was a man who was very severe with himself. Behind the love and gaiety there was a touch of austerity, and he could be severe with others if need be. " Those kindly eyes," says Holland, " could shine with a glint of steel, and the level brows, with their bushy eyebrows, could wear a look of sternness."

He was strict with himself, strong with others, and exceedingly intelligent. Dr. Brightman says, " Those who knew him will perhaps think that he was one of the most intellectual persons they had ever known, only as was perhaps the case with St. Anselm, to whom he has been compared, his intelligence was so much a part of his character, so wholly himself, that it might easily escape notice in the simplicity and charm of his personality."

King always lived in beautiful places, Cuddesdon, Oxford, Lincoln, and with delightful people for his intimate circle, but when a hardship came he always accepted it simply as the next thing to be encountered. He had had a presentiment for years that he would die at forty-two. On his forty-second birthday a tramp was seized with smallpox at Cuddesdon, and died quickly. No man would go near the man or the body. King tended him, lifted the poor, terrible body in his arms, laid it in the coffin, and fastened the coffin down and buried it, feeling that perhaps it was to this that the presentiment had pointed; but he was quite untroubled and he took no harm.

Soon after he became Bishop of Lincoln, a young man lay under sentence of death in the prison, and the chaplain broke down. The Bishop took his place, and visited the man daily. He found he knew nothing of religion. He taught him the Faith, confirmed him, and on the morning of the execution gave him his first and last communion. Afterwards the poor lad came and knelt down by the Bishop, who spoke strong words to him and gave him his blessing. Then he went with him to the scaffold and stood by his side when he died.

Some years afterwards he had to perform the same office for another poor man. King shared all the reticence of English thought about the Saints and their present relation to us, and in a touchingly humble sentence he writes to a friend that he could not help asking for the prayers of Richard, the first criminal he had helped at his end, to help him with this case, and that he felt it to be God's will that he should.

Between Cuddesdon and Lincoln there was the wonderful stretch of years at Oxford when, as Regius Professor of Pastoral Theology, the undergraduates crowded round him in hundreds. I see him now as he sat in the window of his Christ Church study in his cassock, with the light of an October evening falling on him, talking to me about Oxford life in my freshman term.

" There is, of course," he said, " a godless, disorderly strain up here among the men. You will find them

217

in your college and, if they are the leading set there, it is a serious matter, but remember there is a great deal of good among them. It is all there, dear fellow, it is all there, closed up like a tight bud in early spring, only wanting some sunshine and some rain to unfold into the flower." He was, as Holland says, an undying optimist about all men and all things, and that is why an Oxford man could say, " Whenever I saw him in the pulpit I wanted to be good, and I knew I could be."

But the charm of pure goodness is its lightness and gaiety. King won the wayward by the lightness of his touch and captured hearts by his natural fun. A rather tiresome student who was over-fasting in Holy Week got a little note from the Principal. " Dearest man, do eat some breakfast, and come down to the level of your affectionate E. K."

When the present Archbishop of York, Dr. Cosmo Gordon Lang, then the Presbyterian Fellow of All Souls, whom we all designated for the woolsack, decided to take orders in the Church of England, he was sent up to Lincoln to be helped and taught by the Bishop. Mr. Lang arrived at the palace in the middle of dinner, during a Retreat before ordination. He was shown in silence to a seat on the Bishop's right, and joined the solemn and silent dinner listening to a holy book read by a chaplain, the Letters, let us say, of St. Theodore of the Studium. Mr. Lang's heart, he tells us, sank. This, he thought, is the atmosphere into which I am plunging. Presently the Bishop caught his eye, and leaning over, said behind his hand, " We ain't so good as we looks." The neophyte's apprehensions vanished.

There came a day when, arraigned by the Church

Association, he stood at the bar before the Archbishop of Canterbury on the charge of breaking the law of this Church and Realm. His friends noticed afterwards that this had aged him, but his serenity of mind and heart seemed untroubled through all the strain. The practices with which he was charged are now the ordinary practice of what are called Moderate Church-men.

And yet it may be thought that a life lived in such beautiful places which diffused such love and was surrounded by such love, must have been less deeply marked with the cross than the lives of Lowder and Dolling. That was not the case. King's love for all men and all things did not conceal from him the sins and sorrows of the world ; it gave him the most subtle, deep-reaching perception of them.

It was not when He was face to face with Caiaphas or Pilate or the angry mob that our Lord endured the bloody sweat, it was in the moonlit silence of the garden which He loved.

And as we see our dear Bishop of Lincoln, towards the end, sitting in his purple cassock (an old clergyman from the fens had remarked how friendly it had been of his Lordship to receive him in his dressing gown !), when we see him sitting in the evening light in his purple cassock in the big bow window of his study in the old palace, his eyes now resting on the flowers, now following the birds, now gazing wistfully across the smoke-wreathed depths in which his city lay to the hills beyond, we realize that the less tangible a spiritual burden is the more oppressive it can be, and that if one loves this world as King loved it one must always share something of Gethsemane, because it was love grappling in thought with sin which drew the bloody sweat.

No ! such as King always live here *in via*, not yet *in patria ;* that is still to come.

" This world is the place to make friendships," says the Bishop ; " it is in the next that we shall really enjoy them " ; and with these words he waves to us now one of his radiant good-byes.

ARTHUR STANTON

" Now when Jesus was in Bethany in the house of Simon the Leper there
came unto Him a woman having an alabaster box of very precious ointment
and poured it on His head as He sat at meat.   But when His disciples saw
it they had much indignation saying, To what purpose is this waste ? "
St. Matt. xxvi, 6, 7, 8.

THE scene is the first-floor landing of a staircase at
Rugby. The best-looking boy in the school stands
with his hands in his pockets. He has a powerful
voice and is consequently known to the school as the
Scranker.

The Scranker's study is being moved to an upper
floor, and the agonizing moment has been reached when
the sofa appears to decline to go round the curve of the
staircase. His school-fellows used to say that the
Scranker had a rum way of seeming to be looking at
something a long way off. On this occasion he is
concentrated on the agitating foreground. At last the
sofa kindly relents and disappears aloft, followed by the
benediction of the Scranker, " Sofa—r, so good."

The text I have chosen was the text of the first sermon
I ever heard the Scranker preach, and I have chosen it
because it tells us in a phrase the story of the Scranker's
life.

Arthur Stanton was one of the beautiful creatures of
this world. Through that splendidly moulded head

and face poised on that tall and manly body there gradually shone out an enchanting personality.

His colleague, Edward Russell, was one of the most fastidious of men ; it was easy to offend the taste of Russell, but the spell of fascination which Stanton laid on Russell never weakened through all the years. Of all the beautiful products of nature or of art which Russell admired, his wonderful brother priest came first. I have never seen an actor who could compare with Stanton for physical beauty, and although he was the simplest of men and would have repudiated with laughing scorn what I am saying about him, there is no doubt that he had the temperament, mind and power of a consummate artist. Had he entered the theatrical profession, with his physical beauty, his power of expression, his compass of voice, and the spiritual perception which lay behind them, he would have been one of the greatest actors of any age.

Stanton came of a well-to-do Gloucestershire family ; his father died when he was young, so he was always a man of independent means. He had all the acute sensitiveness of the artistic temperament. He was over-sensitive ; it was his besetting fault. He was acutely sensitive to personal opposition ; he was inclined to be sensitive to pain and discomfort. He was extremely sensitive to climate : his barometer and his thermometer were his hobbies, and a standing joke among his brother priests ; he had a passion for watching the sky and the clouds ; there is a seat on the staircase of the St. Alban's Clergy House on which he used to sit peering up into what he could see of the murky London sky. In fact he was to other men what that costly, graceful vessel of fragrant perfume was to the other vessels in the supper room at Bethany, and like that vessel he gave himself to be broken and poured out upon the Saviour's head and feet in a London slum.

I take Stanton to-night therefore as illustrating one of the elements in the morale of a true Anglo-Catholic movement. He illustrates the fact that it must exhibit the consecration—I should have said the sacrifice—of all natural gifts to the service of the Lord Jesus Christ.

The artistic temperament and an artistic gift bring pain and sacrifice into the life of their possessor. If the gift is of the highest quality it is rarely recognized at first ; often its owner, like the Supreme Artist Himself, Jesus Christ, is despised and rejected of men, and always it is with travail that its fruits are borne. But all artistic gifts are divine, and they never manifest themselves in the completeness of their naturalness and power unless they are used as His instruments by the servants of God.

Stanton lived a life of sacrifice, and therefore his natural gifts did the greatest work of all ; they saved souls.

Many of you knew something of Father Stanton in his later days, the days when he was immovably fixed at St. Alban's. Some of you used to help to crowd St. Alban's on his Monday evenings ; some of you used to wedge yourselves in to assist at the Three Hours when he preached it. You saw him get up, open a Bible, and he always suggested to you the preciousness of the Bible by the way he turned over the pages ; then he found his text, or rather discovered it, and began with a sort of hesitating, adventurous air to explore its meaning ; then he would pounce on its meaning and gather it all up and soar away and carry you with him, now laughing, now crying, always rigidly absorbed and thrilled, thrilled as you are thrilled not by argument but by music. It was a gift of using speech like music which Stanton had. He could suggest things to you which he did not say and which are incapable of statement. I daresay you thought it was all a spontaneous effort, that it gave him no trouble at all. No, the whole sermon had been carefully thought out, analysed, written out fair in a note-book, not learned, but entirely absorbed, and then put forth as the deliberate message of the preacher. Every sermon of Stanton's was the deliberately offered sacrifice of his consummate gift to Our Lord.

For the rest, you loved the man's personality, and delighted in collecting funny stories about him and his adventures with the people in the slums.

I once tried to get him to come to Oxford to speak to undergraduates. I got a crushing reply. " My dear Mackay, I can't lecture a hang, and *I don't really* think the fellows would care a hang. It would be dismalissimus. This is really why I think I can't come. It's a matter of common sense and no kid at all about it."

I waited a term or two and then got some undergraduates to ask him, and he came like a shot. There was a tremendous pack all agog for Stanton's stories. Stanton asked for a Bible, found a text, and preached a heart-searching sermon on the Precious Blood. Afterwards he told the men to stand, and then he prayed in his own words that they might know the love of the

Lord Jesus and the power of His Blood. Then he sat down, and there was an appalling silence for a long time until someone in desperation said, "Will you tell us something about your work?"

"About St. Alban's?" said Stanton. "Oh, yes, of course," and kept them all for over an hour between laughter and tears.

The man who described the meeting says, "It lives in my mind out of all the meetings I have ever been to as the one meeting to which I am enormously thankful to have gone."

I am not going to tell you funny stories about Stanton or funny stories Stanton told : I am going to tell you the story of Stanton himself. I am going to explain to you *why* you could always find him at St. Alban's, and this is not at all a funny story.

Stanton sacrificed all his prospects in life, not like Lowder and Dolling for the sake of Christ in His Poor, but for the sake of Christ in His Church. He loved the poor ; if he had been forbidden to exercise his priesthood he meant to go and live as an artisan in the slums, but among my six worthies he stands out as the confessor for the Faith.

Every great artist has a great ideal, a great love. The love of Stanton's life was the love of Jesus and Mary, who from his earliest childhood spoke to him and helped him through the Catholic tradition. The artist in him recognized that Catholic Faith and Practice is the Divinely ordained expression in this world of Jesus, His Mother and His Saints. Those who attacked Catholic Faith and Practice in Stanton's eyes attacked the home of Jesus and Mary, obscured their manifestation, and thwarted their work for men. He defended Catholic Faith and Practice therefore as a man defends his spouse and his home.

When he was at Oxford he went to St. George's-in-the-East to help Lowder and Mackonochie in the riots. Once, when the Protestants made a rush at the altar to destroy it, Stanton in cassock and surplice threw himself in front of it and stood there with folded arms facing the mob. The mob dared not touch him, the altar was saved. That remained his life-long attitude.

He went to Cuddesdon at the time when Bishop Wilberforce was trying to make it more Low Church. He found that Catholic acts of devotion were being discouraged, and asked Liddon what he should do. Liddon advised a measure of conformity, but said, " On no account should I rise from my knees while any of the Consecrated Elements were unconsumed, either at the time of Communion or at the conclusion of the service. To do so would be to imply that you believed only in a Presence in the soul of the receiver, and those who know how much depends upon the revealed truth that our Lord is present in and under the sacramental elements after Consecration whether He is received or no, could never consent to let the point appear to be one of indifference."

Stanton had been profoundly impressed by the zeal, the fervour, and the Scottish courage and calm of Mackonochie. Mackonochie was about to form the parish of St. Alban's in the slums of Holborn, and Stanton accepted his invitation to join him. He mentioned his intention while still at Oxford to Dr. Tait,

Bishop of London. "If you go to Mackonochie at St. Alban's," said the Bishop, "you must never expect any Church preferment." Stanton went.

Mackonochie had begun his services in a room over a costermonger's fish shop, but he had now moved them to a cellar in Greville Street. The only light came through a grating in the pavement, the coal-hole was the vestry, and in this cellar Stanton preached his first sermon while his parishioners cat-called at him down the coal-shoot.

That the boy knew what he was in for is plain from the text he chose to have painted over his chimney-piece in the new clergy house : " There remaineth therefore a rest for the people of God."

His preaching power appeared at once ; from the first he was magnetic, at once he preached Jesus, and the people began to crowd. One of his dodges when taking a mission was to stand at a street corner in a cassock and biretta, and toss his surplice up into the air. If you saw a gloriously beautiful young man playing ball with a surplice you would feel obliged to investigate the matter ; so did the crowd, and then Stanton got on a stool and preached Jesus to them. He was very soon denounced ; somebody complained to the Bishop that Stanton confessed to Mackonochie every day, and carried the Blessed Sacrament about in his pocket. Tait pooh-poohed the rubbish, and said to Stanton, " Remember, they are watching you."

Stanton began by doing the sort of work Father Vernon is doing now, preaching big missions about England. Some of his earliest missions were to soldiers, and had the most wonderful results. My tale will tell you how all his missions were put to an end.

In 1866 came the great attack on the Anglo-Catholics by Lord Sidney Godolphin Osborne in *The Times*. The second great attack, you remember, came in 1899, when Sir William Harcourt attacked us in the same journal. The Public Worship Regulation Act was the result of the first attack, the revised Prayer Book is the long-delayed result of the second.

In the general *mêlée* which followed the attack of 1866, St. Alban's, Holborn, became the storm centre. The Protestants astutely saw that the moral weight of a successful Catholic work among the poor was greater than that of a church frequented by the well-to-do. No doubt it was felt also that the attractive young Stanton must be got rid of, but that could only be done by attacking his Vicar.

The storm began by the Chaplain-General forbidding Stanton to have anything further to do with soldiers, and by the Bishop giving the Church Association leave to attack Mackonochie.

Mrs. Stanton, of Upfield, was deeply distressed that her Arthur should be involved in such matters, and remonstrated with him pathetically. Stanton's letters show the love and the firmness of a St. Francis de Sales.

" My dear Mother,

I am a Catholic in heart, longings and hopes. Catholics believe, as they believe in their God, that Jesus Christ is present on His Altar in the Holy Sacrament. A Catholic priest believes that he holds between his hands the Blood of Life ; as St. John says he handled the Word of Life with his hands. I hold the doctrine of the Real Presence dearer than life. As I hope for salvation I would rather be hacked to pieces than omit adoring my God in the Sacrament."

About the same time, Stanton wrote to his sister, " I go to Shepperton this week to preach for a dear old Evangelical Calvinist. I am sure we shall get on, as he loves Jesus."

After a long delay the courts forbade the St. Alban's clergy to elevate, genuflect, use incense, mix the chalice and burn altar lights.

Mackonochie thought he must submit in some particulars. Stanton did not. " In the name of the God of justice," he said, " let us resist this tyranny tooth and nail."

Mackonochie gave up lighting the candles, and Stanton bought seven lamps to burn instead. " Following the example," he writes, " of Mr. Richards of All Saints', Margaret Street, we shall be more explicit in future in teaching the doctrine of the Mass."

But Mackonochie had not pacified his opponents, because he would not give up the adoration of our Lord in the Holy Sacrament. He was summoned before the courts again, and this time suspended for three months. On the first Sunday he sat in his stall unable to say Mass or to preach, while Stanton thundered on the subject from the pulpit. Not long after this the courts in Mr. Bennett's case decided that the doctrine of the Objective Presence in the Blessed Sacrament was, after

all, permissible in the Church of England. On which
Stanton wrote, " I see Mr. Bennett's case is given for
him. I am glad only because if people prosecute they
should pay for it. It does not matter in the least to
me whether the law says Christ is in the Sacrament or
not. *He is*, and that is all I care about."

Years went on during which Stanton was wholly
engaged in preaching the Gospel, ministering in the
confessional, and doing social work of various kinds ;
but in 1875 he found himself temporarily in charge of
St. Alban's. The tireless Church Association had
managed to get Machonochie suspended for six weeks.
He went abroad, and the Bishop of London told Stanton
that he was to celebrate next Sunday in a surplice only,
not even a stole, and must use common household bread.
Stanton put up a notice : " N.B. There will be no
celebration of Holy Communion in this church until
further notice. All other services as usual." And
next Sunday he marched the whole congregation off to
St. Vedast's, Foster Lane, where Father Hogg sang
Mass in the usual way. The Bishop stopped this by
prohibiting the clergy of St. Alban's to officiate in any
church where the vestments were used, but the congregation continued to go off to St. Vedast's once
Stanton's sermon was finished, until Mackonochie
came back. When Mackonochie returned *Missa Cantata*
was resumed at St. Alban's.

But this decisive action of Stanton's changed the
whole course of his life and the character of his ministry.
When he was advertised to take Missions bishop after
bishop inhibited him from preaching in his diocese.
After 1875 Stanton's *urbi et orbi* ministry was at an end,

for the remaining thirty-eight years of his life, although he preached here and there for friends in dioceses where he had not been inhibited, he regarded his Anglican ministry as closed except at St. Alban's itself. He was perfectly happy in his work, but he felt he had been rejected by the Church of England. When he was dying he was offered a Prebendal stall in St. Paul's, but he refused it with a grateful acknowledgment of the kindness of the offer.

But there was one honour, however, he could not refuse. He could not stop London giving him a public funeral. The complete sacrifice of this man of such wonderful beauty and power to his convictions in a life-long service of God and man brought the whole of London to his grave. From St. Alban's to Waterloo Station amid dense and silent masses of bareheaded Londoners, his brother priests, now old, old men, walked with the little hand bier between them on which his body lay. When they got across the bridge the crowds on the Surrey shore began the Easter hymn :

> The strife is o'er, the battle done ;
> Now is the Victor's triumph won ;
> O let the song of praise be sung,
> Alleluia.

I stood at the corner of Wellington Street and the Strand that day, and saw the little hand-barrow wheeled down past the portico of the Lyceum Theatre, sacred to me with memories of great Shakespearean nights, amid those vast multitudes, and the scene lit up for me a Gospel story. For here was one who as a young man had kneeled at Jesus' feet and said to Him, " Good Master, what shall I do to inherit eternal life ? " and

Jesus, looking upon him, had loved him and said, " Go, sell all that thou hast, and give to the poor, and thou shalt have treasure in heaven, and come, follow Me." And the young man was glad at that saying and he had come with joy, having sold all that he had, for he had great possessions, and he had followed Jesus in the Way.

RICHARD MEUX BENSON

" O God, Thou art my God, early will I seek Thee, my soul thirsteth for Thee, my flesh also longeth after Thee in a barren and dry land where no water is."—*Psalm* lxiii. 1.

I have been speaking of the *morale* of the Anglo-Catholic movement. We have seen that it must be inspired by a thirst for souls as Charles Lowder was ; that it must wage war against oppression and wrong as Robert Dolling did ; that it must see and love the best in all men after the example of Edward King ; that it must consecrate in sacrifice all natural gifts with the simplicity and completeness of an Arthur Stanton.

I now ask you to realize that it must see the highest vision of life known to men, and must furnish men and women who pursue that life—the life of the Evangelical Counsels of Perfection.

Perhaps the clearest proof of all that the Anglo-Catholic movement really deserves the name of Catholic is that it has produced such a life as that of Richard Benson, the Founder of the Society of St. John the Evangelist, popularly known as the Society of the Cowley Fathers.

I have to try to speak now about that ideal of life which is technically called the Religious Life.

By the Religious Life we mean a life seeking personal perfection through a completeness of union with God.

We all possess this inclination, although it is hindered and can be destroyed by many things, but all over the world in all the great religions there is a strain of people in whom it overmasters all other inclinations. The technically religious life appears in all the great religions. But the Catholic religious life is superior to all others in truth, in sanctity, and in fruitfulness. It is based upon Holy Scripture.

If we ask Holy Scripture in what perfection consists, it tells us that it consists in a charity which finds its source and motive in God and its opportunities amongst our neighbours.

The obstacle, says the New Testament, to the attainment of perfect charity, is a disordered desire for created things, and the New Testament counsels us to be detached from all hindrances to perfect charity. It counsels the renunciation of riches ; it counsels the renunciation of carnal pleasures ; it counsels the renunciation of self-seeking in a voluntary submission to, and a generous devotion to, the service of God and man.

Now all Christians are bound to live in this spirit, but a literal fulfilment of these counsels is not intended for all men, is not possible for all men. A certain handling of wealth, a certain use of the instincts of the body, a certain use of rank and power are necessary to a continuance of the human society which our Lord came to redeem and sanctify, and not only are these tolerated by Christianity, but in the Sacraments of Matrimony and Holy Order they are made instruments of God Himself.

But as one among a variety of Christian careers, there

234

stands first and highest the profession and practice of the Evangelical counsels in their literal sense.

The men and women who profess and practise the Evangelical counsels are not *ipso facto* more perfect men and women than others, but they have adopted the best method of perfection. The final object of their lives, their final destiny, are the same as those of others, but they are charged with a particular duty, the duty of reminding others of that destiny and of the means of fulfilling it, and in the scheme of justice they pay for this honour with the sacrifices it entails.

The two prominent counsels of perfection in the New Testament are poverty—" Sell all that thou hast, "and chastity—" There are eunuchs that have made themselves eunuchs for the Kingdom of Heaven's sake. He that is able to receive it let him receive it." But these are negative and there remains the positive pursuit of the charity of Christ in a life wholly devoted to God and one's neighbour, either in prayer and contemplation or in active works of mercy. Such a life must be lived under obedience to religious authority.

In the highest life of all the will of religious authority must override the personal will, because there would be no completeness in the sacrifice if the goodwill itself were not sacrificed with all else.

And so we get our vision of what the Catholic Church calls the life of the counsels or the religious life. It has three elements :

First—the three Evangelical counsels, Poverty, Chastity and Obedience.

Secondly—since it exists to be a light to the world

and not for the spiritual satisfaction of its possessors, the External Profession of the counsels.

Thirdly—since its value lies in perseverance, in its being a fixed and permanent state, not only an internal profession of the counsels, but a vow to their perpetual profession.

I am now going to speak to you about the man who stands before the Church as the leading embodiment of the life of the counsels in the Anglo-Catholic Movement, the founder of the first order of Clerks Regular (for that is the proper technical description of the Society of St. John the Evangelist) in the Church of England since the Reformation.

Richard Benson was not the pioneer in order of time. When we remember that there stood by the Cross of Jesus His Mother, we are not surprised that it was a daughter of Mary who first took the vows of Holy Religion among us. Marian Hughes, afterwards Mother Superior of the Society of the Holy and Undivided Trinity, made her religious profession on Trinity Sunday, 1841, and between that date and the profession of Father Benson, Father Grafton and Father O'Neill in 1866, very many of our great orders of women religious arose—St. Thomas ; Wantage ; All Saints' ; Clewer ; East Grinstead ; Holy Cross ; St. Peter's, Horbury ; St. Peter's, Kilburn ; the Holy Name ; the Sisters of Bethany ; and many others. But when a strong and growing body of Regular Priests appeared, ob- viously possessed by the true motive and spirit of the religious life, it was natural for the other communities to turn to them for example and help, and so inevitably Cowley has found itself inspiring and guiding the growth of the religious life amongst us, and pointing the way for the communities of men which have arisen since, the Order of the Holy Cross in America, the Community of the Resurrection, the Oxford Mission to Calcutta, the Society of the Sacred Mission, and the revivals of the Franciscan and Benedictine Rules.

Richard Benson was the son of wealthy parents, and in spirit and desire was, like St. John the Baptist, a religious from the beginning of his life. When he was a small boy his governess, going into the nursery one night, found Richard's cot empty and the child fast asleep on the ground. She put him back into his cot and told him he must not do such a thing again. " But how am I to learn to be hard if I may not sleep on the floor ? " said the little boy.

After a period of foreign travel in which the youth saw much interesting society, and had a private audience of Pope Gregory XVI, he went to Christ Church. He took a double second in Greats and Mathematics, and in the year after he obtained the Kennicott Hebrew Scholarship and was appointed a Senior Student, what other colleges call a Fellow, of Christ Church. After his degree in 1847 he was ordained curate of Surbiton, where he gave very large sums of money to the new church. Three years later, Christ Church gave him the country living of Cowley, a small village two and a half miles from Oxford, with a parish which extended to Magdalen Bridge. No Vicar had resided at Cowley for a long time ; one of the Senior Students of Christ Church used to ride out on Sundays and take two services there.

For nine years Benson—who was an embodiment of

the devotion, reserve, austerity and self-effacement of the Tractarians—lived there unobserved, in prayer and labour among the poor. He felt towards the close of the time a call to missionary work, and set his heart on India. All his plans were made and he was on the point of leaving England, when the Bishop of Oxford intervened. He begged Benson to remain and deal with the large new suburb of Oxford which was growing up on the Cowley side of Magdalen Bridge. This was the great act of renunciation of Benson's life. When he gave up India for Cowley St. John, he gave to God all he was and all he cared for, and by doing so found a point of entrance for the religious life into the modern Church of England. Bishop Wilberforce was able to countenance it, because he saw that there was a complete absence of self-will in the life and plans of the founder.

Benson built an iron church in the new suburb, and settled into lodgings in the Iffley Road.

Anything more drab and humdrum after his high Indian hopes cannot be imagined. But he had his reward. From that spot he afterwards planted two branches of his Order in India, with two others in America and South Africa. For gradually his call to the Religious Life became clear to Benson. A priest named Grafton came over from America to consult Dr. Pusey, with the same hope in his heart. Pusey sent him to Benson. And in 1866, Benson, Grafton, and a priest called O'Neill, after a year of spiritual preparation, and having obtained the sanction and benediction of the bishop of the diocese, took the vows and formed the Society of St. John the Evangelist. Soon after Oliver Prescott joined them. It was all most simple and most real. They lived crowded together in a little suburban brick house in the Iffley Road. They said the Day Hours in a tiny oratory, and Mass and the Prayer Book Offices in the parish church. In 1868 the old red-brick mission-house was opened with its bare, bleak chapel perched up on the roof ; the chapel had ugly brown-painted deal-fittings, and a severe Byzantine mosaic over the altar. There was nothing naturally attractive about it, it was an embodiment in brick and wood of poverty and detachment, like San Damiano and the Carceri, but planted in an ugly English midland suburb with none of the Italian charm.

In 1870, four novices joined the first group, one of whom became the second Superior-General, Father Page. From this time the activities of the Society became many and great. Priests were gathered into the chapel for Retreats, and every effort was made to deepen the spiritual life of the clergy. The Fathers went out on Missions in all directions. For many years the Society slowly shaped its constitution, testing it by the experience of time, and in 1884 Bishop Mackarness, of Oxford, confirmed it, and the Society became an order of clerks regular, in the manner prescribed by Catholic precedent.

At last we come to the man and his life. *Benson's mission was to embody the spirit of the religious life in such a way that men might understand, and that those who were called might follow.* To do this he had to be without natural attractiveness, there had to be as little of him beyond the spirit as possible.

Benson had no form or comeliness apart from the tranquil shining spirit which shone through his dim

short-sighted eyes, and in the strong, benevolent lines
of his mouth. A little shrivelled, bent, thin, wiry,
ascetic figure, full of energy, often looking as though he
were concealing physical suffering but at fitting times
brimming over with laughter and humour, a shabby,
faded cassock, a neck-cloth renewed not very often,
stockingless feet thrust into old shoes, the cassock
girded very tightly—that is the figure people remember,
a harsh, rather hesitating voice, no power of popular
preaching, nothing to attract you short of the highest
characteristics of all.

But then those ! The motive of Father Benson's
life was union with the most Holy Trinity in Unity.
That was his passion. His thirst for souls, his battle
against wrong, his love of all men, his consecration of
the material were all elements, necessary elements in
his passion for God.

God with him was indeed central and supreme, and
the externals he valued, the letter of Holy Scripture,
the precise use of prayer, the practice of the Sacraments,
had their value strictly and only to him as means to the
knowledge of God, means to union with God.

In this also lay to him the whole meaning of the vows
of the Religious Life. Through them the soul is dedicated with the greatest possible completeness. Father
Benson was vowed to poverty and chastity because these
were instruments for a clear vision of God and a closer
conformity to His Will ; humility and obedience were
to him the necessary consequence of the attitude the
creature must hold towards the Creator.

You see then that this was the man raised up to gain
entrance again for the religious life into the English

world. We often hear of the utility of the religious life and its economy, but such notions of it wholly misunderstand it. Father Benson was raised up to make it clear that the religious life is a response to a divine vocation ; that its motive is a simple and absolute surrender of self with all one has or is to God, to live in close and undisturbed fellowship with Him after the example and in obedience to the counsels of His Incarnation.

"He always seemed to me," said Bishop Churton, "more full of the supernatural holiness and power which come from divine grace acting on a wholly surrendered life than anyone I ever saw." And this being so we are not surprised to hear of the supernatural power which shone through his meditations in the month's retreat of the Society in its early days.

Father Maturin, writing years after he became a Roman Catholic, said that these addresses were inspiring beyond anything he ever heard before or since, that all harshness and hesitation disappeared, the modulations of the father's voice became like music, and his language and diction perfect, while the words came with a curious air of detachment. "For fertility, originality of thought and the abundant gift of expression and illustration I have never," says Father Maturin, "heard the equal of those addresses."

"It was," says another father, "the most intimate outpouring of a soul in communion with God, an inspired word indeed, and I suppose what St. Paul meant by the gift of prophecy."

In fact, that austere little upper chamber at Cowley witnessed scenes of the apostolic power of the first days.

Father Congreve, speaking of his Superior with that subtle discernment of which he was master, says that Father Benson's austerity was so much part of himself that it became a hardy soldier's indifference rather than a virtue consciously acquired. He was untouched by self-consideration, self-pity, self-indulgence.

Few people since the days of the Patriarchs can have had so long a conscious life as Father Benson, for he lived to ninety-one, and was awake eighteen or twenty hours out of the twenty-four during most of his life. He worked all day, except during the prescribed half-hours of recreation, and the greater part of every night. He often went to bed at four, and not infrequently he did not go to bed at all. His power of fasting was extraordinary. Up to nearly the end of his life he did not eat or drink between Maundy Thursday and dinner-time on Easter Day. Bishop Hall says that once Benson was suffering severely from a bad carbuncle, and his head and one eye had to be bandaged up. In this condition he preached the University sermon at Oxford fasting, and then returned to Cowley and sang High Mass.

" Extraordinary," you say. Yes, I am afraid so, in the service of Christ, but not at all extraordinary in the service of England, France and Germany during the Great War.

Father Benson insisted that great self-sacrifice belongs to ordinary Christianity. We give ourselves to God in every sacrament, in every prayer, and we live the rest of our lives to carry out the sacrificial gift of ourselves to God to completeness. What can be simpler ?

A terrible ideal, you think ? I have just been reading *The Great Days of Versailles*, by Mr. Bradby. Poor

Louis the Fourteenth ! Father Benson enjoyed earthly life far more than he did. " Vanity of vanities, all is vanity " should be carved upon the portals of Versailles.

Listen to this for an ending. It is written on the Atlantic to one of the fathers : " We are just off Sandy Hook, the voyage has been beautiful. Several times I have been able to say the office with porthole open and my face towards the great expanse of waters, the waters below the firmament, the waters of the mid-heavens, and high, unseen, the glorious water of the bow like unto an emerald and the solid glassy sea like unto crystal, no longer moving like the wide waste below, but established in the accomplished truth and perfected in the bright purity of the throne of God. Since St. Simon and St. Jude's day I have been keeping the voyage in active company with King David, and learning some little more of the delight of that inexhaustible treasury.

" How strange it is to think that one can have such an intense secret of happiness ! It makes one wonder why God should have been pleased to reveal such a delight to oneself. One ought to be very thankful."

FRANK WESTON

" I am already being offered and the time of my departure is come."—
II *Timothy* iv. 6 (*R. V.*).

MANY scholars think that St. Paul did not write these words, that a disciple wrote them under the authority of his name. Whoever wrote them, they show the relation of such a life as St. Paul's to the death which closes it here. The death is the final act in this world of a long series of acts, the act in which the witness of the life is consummated and crowned.

The morale of a true Anglo-Catholic movement involves faithfulness unto death. That that fact must be illustrated before this series ends is plain, and I take Frank Weston as illustrating it because he and the trials of his life do this in such a strikingly pictorial way.

Frank Weston was born of good stock. He appears first as a little boy in suburban middle-class surroundings, an affectionate, diffident, delicate child, very highly strung. His nerves bothered him all his life, his courage was not natural to him, but was the result of a disciplined will. He had an Evangelical upbringing and a beautiful mother. All these six men were the gifts to the Church of holy mothers. Mothers, mark this ! Meant for the Army, he failed to pass the eye test at Woolwich.

That was the first stroke of his discipline ; he felt it keenly. Weak sight hindered his reading and baulked his games. In all this, I expected the big round-shouldered, short-sighted, ·rather awkward Dulwich schoolboy was going through much more self-discipline than people knew. We are told that he went up to Trinity College, Oxford, old for his age, solemn, shy, and rather repelling in manner, all signs of inward suffering.

"Honestly," he said afterwards, "I have never conceived it possible that anyone would care to like me." With this agonizing diffidence about himself he combined an almost aggressive certainty about the validity of his beliefs.

But as often happens, the awkward, uncomfortable freshman found himself at Oxford, and grew into a keen, attractive, thoughtful, serious undergraduate. He and his friends formed a debating society, the Moles, and debated all subjects under the sun. Frank became a Christian Socialist, squabbled with my brother Librarian at Pusey House, John Carter, for his cautiousness, and enrolled himself in Stewart Headlam's more militant band.

Then came a great night when Bishop Smythies, of Zanzibar, king among men, stood in the pulpit of St. Barnabas, and pleaded for Africa. Weston volunteered next day and was turned down by the doctor.

He spent only three years in Oxford, reading theology, overworked desperately, got a good First in the schools, and went to the College Mission at Stratford.

The knight-errant in him was taking shape, and he

went down to the East End in the spirit of joyous adventure. Here his powers of leadership began to appear. He had a strong, quiet manner which won the confidence of the bigger boys who called him the Cardinal and made him their confidant. It was a glorious time of Christian Socialism and growing Anglo-Catholicism until the Protestant Conservative element at Oxford intervened, and Frank Weston resigned the college mission and went to St. Matthew's, Westminster. Two sayings had always stuck in his mind. When he was a boy at Dulwich, the Headmaster, who had a curious power of divination, one day said to him, à propos of nothing, " Weston, if Jesus Christ asked you to give Him your overcoat would you go and fetch Him your shabbiest ? " Weston said, " No, sir," and he proved as good as his word. And when he was at Stratford and was talking one night in Oxford the socialistic doctrine which was to " build Jerusalem in England's green and pleasant land," a Don said to him, " Weston, do you believe in the heavenly Jerusalem ? "

" Yes," said Weston.

" I wish I did," said the Don ; " and if I did I don't think I should talk about anything else."

The saying shook Weston's mind into a new perspective. After sorting his ideas, praying and meditating and developing his work as a priest in the orderly devotional atmosphere of St. Matthew's, he volunteered again for Central Africa, was accepted and went out to Zanzibar.

He went out with the highest ideals, and with theories to put to the test of experience. When he got out he found himself dissatisfied at every turn. He thought the life and discipline of the mission relaxed. He was put to train teachers for orders under conditions which he thought impossible. He found a tendency to Europeanize the natives, and he had come out intending to help the natives to found a native Church and develop through its power a native African civilization. Some people would have come home, other people would have submitted, others, again, would have begun to question their own judgment. Weston did none of these things. He attacked everything he objected to and started to build a theological college ; meanwhile the climate found him out, and these excursions and alarums went on amid sharp bouts of fever.

All that side of Weston which had made him a socialist at Stratford gave itself to the Africans. To the Africans he became an African to an extraordinary degree. Not only was he the first Swahili orator and scholar, but he came to think in Swahili, which latterly affected to some extent his English style. Many men who have given themselves to be Africanized have deteriorated, but when he died the British Administrator at Tanga wrote, " I think the Bishop was the very impersonation of our race at the highest to which it can attain."

Weston found his recreation at first in looking after the Small Boys' Home. They were delightful and most affectionate children, and at once he had to face the moral problem in a form which wrung his heart. If you go back from the twentieth century to the first you find yourself in a society where none of the Christian traditions of conduct, conventions and repressions exist. It was not difficult to make these children religious, it was very difficult to keep them at all decent in conduct, and it was immensely difficult to make them see that the one had anything to do with the other.

The Catholic missionary bears in his body the marks of the Lord Jesus. From the children at Kilimani the young missionary began to receive the wound in the Sacred Heart. He led a very ascetic life with his theological students when he got them round him. He found, like St. Francis de Sales, that he must make the Blessed Sacrament the centre of their lives. When he told us that we must fight for our tabernacles he spoke out of this experience. He instituted the service of Benediction which he admitted was a tactical mistake from the point of view of the mission at home, but he said, " Souls must be saved, and no priest out here has sufficient guarantee of long years to allow of his considering tactics." I understand that Benediction is now licensed in many churches throughout the diocese of Zanzibar.

He was constantly being called upon to give missions and retreats, but he said, " Nobody does anything for *me*."

After a while he was made Principal of the elder boys' school at Kiungani. His fellow-priests here, like himself, were anxious to try their vocation for the Religious Life, and they petitioned the Bishop to allow them to do so, but he refused.

Weston was a great success at Kiungani and had happy years there. He dominated the whole place, and the boys were devoted to him. But he returned from furlough to find a sort of revolt going on against his

authority, and a layman in his place. The layman soon
retired, and Weston resumed work, but this was a bitter
trial. The boys had wavered and Weston thought his
fellow-missionaries had been against him. It was not
really so, but he was shy and sensitive and formidable, a
difficult combination. This was a time when he lived
very much to himself among the Africans, but it was all
part of his training. In this Gethsemane he found our
Lord, and from henceforth his special devotion became
the *loneliness of Christ*, and in it he found his way deeper
into the African heart and mind.

The period ended by his being made Canon and Chancellor of the Cathedral, with charge of the educational
work of the diocese, and the duty of lecturing to the
European residents in Zanzibar.

It was after this that he came home to appeal for men,
and made his great speech at the Livingstone Com-
memoration in the Senate House at Cambridge. I
went over from Oxford with some others. It was a
great occasion, the Vice-Chancellor in the chair, the
Archbishop of Canterbury, the Public Orator, many of
the great personages of Cambridge present. Weston's
speech was a wonderful example of the power of the
Holy Spirit when He gets an organ through whom He
can speak. I have never seen an audience more deeply
moved. The Bishop of Manchester, who also went
over from Oxford, says that he was still trembling when
he got into the train to go home. Nothing but the
spirit of a life of martyrdom can so shake strong
men.

After a time Dr. Hine resigned the Bishopric, and in
1908 Frank Weston was consecrated Bishop of Zanzibar.

He landed on November 6th and was enthroned that afternoon. Next day, the Bishop sang Pontifical High Mass, standing facing the congregation with his canons ranged behind in the apse of the basilican cathedral ; before him stretched a brilliant mass of colour, white and black folk mingled together in brilliant garments. Next day, sitting on his throne behind the altar, the Bishop delivered his charge, and on the days following he presided over the Synod. He issued a Pastoral in Swahili to the native people beautifully suggestive of Apostolical times, and soon began his episcopal visitation of the vast tropical diocese on foot ; in one six months he walked nine hundred miles. It was these walks which gave the Bishop that splendid manly dignity and grace which we all admired. The splendid figure, to which we did hero-worship at Congress meetings, was built up and poised by Apostolic labours like those St. Paul describes.

Most of you have read the Bishop's Life. You remember his fight with witchcraft in various forms. In Central Africa you are up against forces, whatever they are, which lie latent and suppressed in countries of the Christian civilization. This contest with the principalities and powers St. Paul talks of drew out forces in the Bishop's personality. Things happened such as are recorded in the lives of saints. After walking all day through country which was leafless, remember, because the sun had withered up the leaves and in which, after rain, the grass grew twelve feet high, the Bishop would pray under the stars half the night. *" Of all that he taught me,"* said a native priest, *" of all that I watched him do, this was the greatest wonder to see how he prayed."*

We are not surprised then at the tale that when he was confronted after Mass by a heathen chief who implored him to pray for rain, he gathered the Christians together and prayed in the presence of the chief, and that day torrential rain fell ; and that when he prayed vehemently by a woman far gone in death, her soul was drawn back and she confessed her sins and was absolved, and then died. When the Catholic life is as strongly developed as it was in Weston, such things, explain them as you will, occur.

As Bishop he became disciplinarian of his people. He sat as judge, heard cases, and imposed public penance, but all the time with such a love of souls that he became the father and consoler of all his black children. There is a story of a rebellious sinner and his excommunication from the altars of the Church. The awful ceremony proceeded, the lighted candles were hurled down on the ground and extinguished, and the Bishop came to the final sentence, " We do hereby cut you off—" and then burst into a torrent of tears, and amid the sobs of the Bishop, priests and people, the church bell tolled out the news that the doom had been pronounced.

A Catholic Bishop must expect to find his work imperilled by the assaults of the Devil ; he ought not to have to encounter the assaults of the Bishops and Priests of his own communion, but such was Bishop Weston's lot, and the result was his battle of Kikuyu and his battle with Modernism.

The Church and the Sacraments were at stake in the Kikuyu controversy, and the Person of our Lord in the controversy with Modernism. The Bishop's contention in the Kikuyu case we know. He won his chief points, and we like to think of his departure from the second Kikuyu Conference to the sound of his opponents' cheers. Weston's presence, speech and charm were irresistible.

With regard to Modernism, Bishop Weston was in a painfully favourable position to see what it might lead to.

The Arabs of Cairo were deluging Zanzibar with proselytising Mohammedan tracts in which they pointed out that the Modernist teachers in England were teaching a doctrine of our Lord's Person indistinguishable from Mohammed's account of it, and that our learned men were now making it perfectly clear that Mohammed had been right all the time and the Church wrong. We may regret the methods with which the Bishop fought the Modernists, we may perhaps think them extravagant or out of date. But this is clear, they made it plain to the slow English mind that modern Christian teaching must be watched.

Then the War broke out, and the Bishop, who was in England, got back to his people, and found himself cut off from the greater part of his diocese, which was in German territory. The disorder which war brings had reached Zanzibar ; two of his native priests had to be deposed for immorality. This nearly broke the Bishop's heart, for he found it to be of long standing and concealed from him by the natives. The Bishop flung himself into the work of the cathedral, saying the Masses, hearing the confessions, preaching most of the sermons. Then came a press gang searching for porters; the natives fled and hid, but the Bishop rose and said,

" I will get you porters if I may command them." He was given leave, and the men flocked to him, Christians, Moslems, heathen. The Bishop drilled them and took them to the mainland. This is a great War tale but it cannot be told now.

" Truly is our Lord Bishop a great man," wrote an African afterwards, " for he came over the sea with us, and when we reached the mainland he marched with us, he slept with us, he ate with us, and when we lay down at night did he not pray with us ? And when we rose in the morning did he not pray with us again ? At the end did he not take us into camp ? Truly he is a great man."

An officer serving with the South Africans once watched the Bishop striking camp and getting his men —he had between two and three thousand under him— into marching order. The officer ran after him and said, " I don't know who you are, Sir, but if you want a job after the war come to me ; we shall not quarrel about terms." He was a mining magnate from the Rand.

The Moslems were affected in another way ; they realized that the Bishop was a Holy Man, such a Holy Man as could lead a Holy War among themselves, and for the first time they got a glimpse of the supernatural character of Christianity.

The war left the Bishop two battles to fight which cost him more than those terrible marches. He fought the people who wanted to return her colonies to Germany, in a pamphlet called the *Black Slaves of Prussia*, and he fought our own countrymen when he thought they were going to press hardly on the natives, in another pamphlet called the *Serfs of Great Britain*. In the end Mr. Winston Churchill issued a despatch which satisfied the Bishop.

Well, that is the man we all loved and admired at our Congress meetings ; that is the man the Anglo-Catholic movement must resemble ; like him it must be persevering and dauntless, and not afraid of making mistakes ; like him it must do well, suffer for it, and take it patiently ; like him it must be great-hearted, whole-hearted, eager-hearted ; like him, to the end of a life of self-sacrifice and many disappointments, it must retain the heart of a child. That is the charm of Frank Weston. He never lost the simplicity and joy of a child. He died on the march, marching and working with the illness on him which caused his death. At last it struck him down, but twice he rose from his death-bed to administer the Sacrament of Confirmation. Next day he could rise no more. It was all very simple, merely the next thing to be done in a life lived to the glory of God. His priests came to him and gave him the last Sacraments, and in four hours he passed away.

" Crowds of people," says the native account, " all crowded up, Christians and those not Christians, that they might see the face of the father for the last time. Then arose an exceedingly great lamentation. It was a wonder.

" Everyone you looked at—he was crying, but we returned to the church afterwards to thank the God who had given us a good father, and had now carried him to a place of greater peace that he might rest from the trouble of the world."

But one of the little black schoolboys of Kiungani, writing of him after his death, had a clearer vision.

"You will know that he is a loving man, for his mouth is always opened ready for laughter, for he is still laughing, and he will laugh for ever."